822·33

KT-489-121

THE MACMILLAN

ADVISORY EDITOR : PHILIP BROCKBANK

Professor of English and
Director of the Shakespeare Institute,
University of Birmingham

GENERAL EDITOR : PETER HOLLINDALE

Senior Lecturer in English and Education,
University of York

MUCH ADO ABOUT NOTHING

Other titles in the series:

THE MACMILLAN SHAKESPEARE

MUCH ADO ABOUT NOTHING

Edited by

Jan McKeith

Macmillan Education

First published 1982

Published by
MACMILLAN EDUCATION LIMITED
Houndmills Basingstoke Hampshire RG21 2XS
and London
Associated companies throughout the world

Printed in Hong Kong

British Library Cataloguing in Publication Data

Shakespeare, William
   Much ado about nothing. – (The Macmillan
   Shakespeare)
   I. Title   II. McKeith, Jan
   822.3'3   PR2828

   ISBN 0-333-28628-6

This edition is for
DOMINIC, CATHARINE, MATTHEW and THOMAS

CONTENTS

ACKNOWLEDGEMENTS

These are inevitably due to all the other editors of the play, past and present; and also to my colleague, Norman Stevenson, for our many discussions and his careful reading of the draft.

INTRODUCTION

GOOD FOR A LAUGH? – SOME PROBLEMS OF COMEDY

It may seem somewhat contradictory to talk of comedy in terms of problems, yet Shakespearean comedy can be difficult to understand. The difficulties arise from several sources, not the least of which is the fact that the play is probably being studied as a text, rather than being seen and heard in performance. While this is clearly stultifying for any drama, it is particularly so for comedy, since a great deal of what is easily accessible as 'comic' to modern audiences exists in action and spectacle, intonation and stress; and there surely can be few things more perplexing than a comedy which does not seem to be funny, but instead threatens to be 'duller than a great thaw' (*Much Ado About Nothing*, II. 1.241).

Other difficulties can arise from preconceived notions about the nature of comedy, and indeed about the nature of drama generally. A contemporary stress on the 'realistic' in television drama, for instance, (currently a main source of dramatic experience for most people) makes unfamiliar the idea of dramatic illusion and the means by which it is created. Such illusion, like a perfected web, fully consistent within itself, holds the play together and carries the audience along in a state of acquiescence to its 'unreality'. Disbeliefs about actual correlations between dramatic and external environments disappear in the face of the deeper realities which the play can be seen to be exploring. The play's surface environment thus acts as the medium for this exploration. Messina, its society and its inhabitants, are factually remote to a contemporary audience, but the environment provides the context, and the society a series of relationships and codes, through which underlying truths may be examined.

Expectations about the term 'comedy' can also be misleading since it is now often thought of as simply a means of entertainment giving rise to laughter. But for the reader, Shakespearean comedy guarantees none of the easy hilarity of a comedy programme, since comedy is more a method of approach than an effect. It is a way of seeing and a means of examining perfectly serious issues; laughter may be made to serve this purpose, certainly, but it does not constitute it. For it works by discovering people's frailties and inadequacies beneath the surface of their aspirations to honour and dignity. And it works simultaneously upon individual absurdities and idiosyncrasies, and upon 'society' which often tries to hide its own pretensions from itself.

Some of these comic discoveries can fairly readily be made at first reading, or in improvised performance; but others require patient study of the language. Some of the points that the first audiences might have been quick to take have now to be coaxed out slowly. This particularly applies to the play's bawdiness, which is used quite specifically, not only for the abundant demonstrations of verbal wit (the surface topic, after all, is courtship, and the wit reflects this), but also for more fundamental reasons, in the demonstration of a double standard within the Messinian society. Bawdiness in this play is thus a means serving the ends of the 'wit-crackers' in an essentially light-hearted manner; at the same time, it serves the ends of the playwright in the exploration and development of an important theme.

THE MEANS OF CRAFT

Much Ado About Nothing has been established as written in 1599, and is classified as one of the 'mature' comedies, by which is meant those written just before the more problematical comedies (like *Troilus and Cressida* and *Measure for Measure*) and before the great tragedies. The whole play, a complex of deceptions, starts to explore a theme which will emerge in tragic environments; indeed, its tragic potential is felt even here in Messina. The deceptions appear in different ways; on the one hand, there is self-deception, and on the other, there are the contrivances designed for the deception of others, which are called 'practices', and recur throughout the plot. These 'practices' seek to manipulate the feelings in a way considered by the practitioner to be desirable, and rely for effectiveness on psychological perceptions about the person to be 'practised upon', in a way that is reminiscent of Jonson's knaves. And directing all the deceptions is of course Shakespeare, working the over-all 'practice' of his dramatic illusion.

Much of the plot itself is derived from various sources, and it is always interesting to see how Shakespeare adapts these elements for his particular designs. The Hero/Claudio story appears in several works which were either contemporary with Shakespeare, or had recently undergone fresh translation. The great Italian poem by Ariosto, *Orlando Furioso* (translated in 1591) contains a story centred around a Hero-figure – Genevra – against whom similar false accusations are made. In this story, though, the main emphasis is on the defeat of the wicked duke, who is much more involved in events than the comparable character of Don John in *Much Ado About Nothing*. Spenser in *The Fairy*

3

Queen (Book II, Canto 4) adapted the story to more tragic effect. From an Italian novella by Bandello (1554) comes another version, in which the Claudio-figure is an honourable soldier who witnesses what he thinks is the infidelity of his lover. This story is set at Messina and contains several familiar names, such as King Piero of Arragon and Lionato.

The most surprising aspect of the source material, however, is that it offers no model for the Beatrice/Benedick story which is the very life of the play. A recent piece of research has suggested a life-model for Beatrice in the sister of the Earl of Essex (one Penelope Devereux), who certainly seems to have had a lively and extremely independent mind. But intriguing as such speculations are, they remain speculations and do not further our appreciation of Shakespeare's art. The relationship between Beatrice and Benedick is used by Shakespeare to put all the other elements in the play in a kind of human perspective and to give them their significance.

But Beatrice and Benedick are not in command of the play's effects. Our responses as audience are manipulated by Shakespeare in ways which produce the play's peculiar kinds of suspense. Our information at many points in the play is in advance of some, if not all, of the characters on stage: for example, we know Don Pedro intends to woo for Claudio, Hero does not; we know Beatrice and Benedick are being deceived, they do not; we know of Dogberry's arrests while Leonato and the others remain ignorant. We even know that from the point of the arrest, the truth will eventually surface. The information we possess serves as a perspective on the action, so that we focus not on 'what will happen next?' as in straight suspense, but on 'when will it happen, and how?' which is the teasing suspense of comedy, giving us a ready appreciation of the dramatic ironies as they happen.

There is thus a considerable variation in the emotions roused by the play which does not move in any predictable progression, and to some extent the alternations between prose and blank verse can be seen as reflecting the changes in mood. Such changes in the text are worth watching; changes from the informal, conversational flexibility and rapid flow of the prose, to the more formal, measured qualities of the blank verse; from the quick-firing of pun and witty repartee, to the elegant imagery and precise metaphor; from lightness or irony in tone, to the more sonorous intonation of distress, or the sharpness of indignant anger.

Early in the play, occasions of verse are rare and therefore marked (for example, Claudio seeking help from Don Pedro, I. 1; and his first dismissal of Hero, II. 1). But as the play, which has begun with effusive, joke-cracking hospitality as well as the taut exchange of rival wits, moves towards the searing unpleasantness of the church scene, blank verse becomes increasingly dominant. First of all, there is the scene where Hero effects the tricking of Beatrice (III. 1) and Hero and Ursula simulate a serious discussion. Hero even suggests the process by which her own reputation is about to be destroyed:

> And truly, I'll devise some honest slanders
> To stain my cousin with. One doth not know
> How much an ill word may empoison liking.
>
> > (III. 1.84–6)

and the use of verse overall here is like a prelude to IV. 1 where the real empoisoning takes effect.

In the last two acts, the moves between verse and prose become more obviously differentiated, in that verse seems reserved for the solemn matters (the main part of IV. 1; Leonato's comfortless distress at V. 1; the scene at Hero's tomb, V. 3) while the prose occurs in more personal or informal contacts (such as the Beatrice/Benedick exchange at the end of IV. 1), and to convey the awkwardness of Don Pedro's and Claudio's search for levity to help them ride over the unpleasant truth of Hero's 'death'. The final scene of general restoration remains in verse until the last wrangle has been resolved, when everyone is allowed back into prose as though confident that all will now be well.

The actual stage environment, in the location of scenes, can also be used to create important unities and contrasts. Early editions did not of course designate these specifically, but much can be derived from an imaginative reading of the text. Beatrice and Benedick can, for instance, overhear the talk about their lovers from the same arbour; the church sees both the denigration of Hero and the beginning of her restoration; the general scene outside Leonato's house which carries the cheerful greeting of visitors at I. 1, is also the background for the grieving father at V. 1.

Added to such effects are contrasts between particular dramatic activities, such as song and dance. The songs reflect the total shift in the play's atmosphere, from the carefree advice of 'Sigh no more, ladies' to the sombre lament at the tomb. The dances, on the other hand, reflect another kind of change: the first shows itself as a fragile and short-lived unity, whilst the second makes lasting conjunctions and provides the play with its final image. As an age-old metaphor for the whole process of courtship (even though it undergoes such reductive analysis by Beatrice at II. 1), the dance is a major symbol in the play. As a social activity, it also makes provision for another dramatic effect in the process of masking, which is in itself a formalisation of a central theme, the deception of appearances.

The early platform stage inevitably made different demands to the modern one and used the minimum of set and props. It also lent itself to a much greater intimacy with the audience, so that the confidentiality of 'asides', for instance, was easier to create, and the scenes where the villains meet could be given a strong visual sense of conspiratorial separation, by being conducted at the very front of the platform. By contrast, major scenes, like the formal denunciations in the church, could be given a dominating central focus.

Any playwright of the time had to take account of the often verbally-responsive audiences. The equivalent of the gallery consisted of the area directly adjacent to the stage, and it is thought that unscripted exchanges between actors and audiences were not uncommon, and by no means always refined. For this reason it might be dramatic wisdom, as well as dramatic economy, to have a tricky scene like Margaret's impersonation of Hero with Borachio played in report only. So much more can be suggested in the discussion of Hero's misdemeanours (note how Don John keeps failing to describe their precise nature and how much he can insinuate by that unspecified disgust) than could have been played out before an observant and perhaps noisy audience. To maintain the full effect of the illusion, as well as providing a means for setting all to rights (in the overheard report), the scene is clearly better played off-stage.

All these aspects help to create and weave a sense of the dramatic fabric as something which exists for a stage, to be seen and heard rather than to be read as a text. But what cannot be described is that which brings the play to life more than the appreciation of these details – the embodiment of characters by actors, whose faces and bodies communicate as much as their tongues. They are the essential element for bringing the play into being, just as the dancer 'creates' the ballet by dancing, or the musician 'creates' music by playing the score. There is no escaping the fact, which in the context of *Much Ado About Nothing* and its themes is something of an irony, that 'believing' comes from seeing; for to see the play in performance transforms our perceptions and renders the illusion whole and comprehensible.

THE ENDS OF PRACTICES

As many have pointed out, plotted and even numbered, the play is riddled with 'practices'. The various deceptions shape the progress of the plot: characters appear to improvise and invent as the occasion demands, and a succession of 'seeming truths' is generated for the purposes of promoting their various designs. The inventiveness is usually seen in process – planning, execution and result – and there is a continual re-grouping of participants, as well as a changing line of 'victims', so that by the end, nearly all the characters have played both roles at one time or another during the play. At the same time, it is interesting to note that it is the secondary characters in the play who organise plans involving the central characters. Claudio, by seeking Don Pedro's assistance, provides the opportunity for his ingenuity (I. 1); Don Pedro exercises this again in the complex preparations for the tricking of Beatrice and Benedick (II. 2); Don John's disaffection is ripe for Borachio's scheme (II. 2); and the whole catastrophe provides the Friar with the opportunity for establishing new priorities (IV, 1).

The audience finds itself tricked too, in that the benign intervention of Don Pedro seems amusing. But when Don John's malignant plans emerge, that initial acquiescence has to be questioned; are manipulations only evil when they are engineered by malice? (Note the subtle contrast between Don Pedro, who 'fashions' his 'practices' and Don John, who 'frames' his villainies.) Do well-motivated 'practices' take unjustifiable risks? The answers perhaps lie in the confusion that is caused by the failure, or rather the over-zealous success, of the first plan, which threatens to cause misery. But nothing daunted by this, Don Pedro proceeds to his next scheme – it is all sport to him, for he wants to play the love-god (II. 1.380). He is also a soldier and used to being in command, so he runs his practices like military operations, proposing to take Hero's hearing prisoner 'with the force/And strong encounter of my amorous tale' (I. 1.319–20), and planning briefing sessions for his assistants (II. 1.362ff).

But his strategies, and indeed everyone else's, can only take effect through the predispositions of the society in which they are to be operated. From the beginning of the play, we are shown a habit of mind which places a ready belief in appearances and surface values. At I. 2, for instance, Leonato acts immediately on hearsay, even though he says 'we will hold it as a dream, till it appear itself'; he plans to prepare Hero for the proposal, and at II. 1 rehearses her openly. At the dance itself, even those who are aware of the scheme are taken in by Don Pedro's attitude to Hero, and Claudio here becomes the victim of the 'practice' which he himself has approved. But he learns nothing by the experience, for when Don John brings the disastrous news, it never occurs to him that he might be the victim of malicious practice, any more than it occurs to that master-mind, Don Pedro. They are both as culpable in their credulity as those on whom they have so accurately operated other 'practices'; the ironies are plain enough.

They are not, however, culpable entirely as individuals; the focus of comedy is also on society and such credulity is the hallmark of this particular society, which is much given to 'noting' – observing, over-hearing, believing what it sees and hears, trusting in surface truths. And as the Elizabethan pronunciation of *nothing* was the same as *noting*, there is clearly a pun in the title which also indicates this theme. The audience can, therefore, be fully sensible of the irony when Claudio bitterly appeals to the congregation (at IV. 1) not to believe what it sees in the appearance of Hero's purity, the 'exterior shows'. While this insight is relevant to everyone in the play, it is a fierce irony that it should be revealed by the man who has himself been persuaded by a 'show of truth' (Don John's plot) into making false accusations. Don John has truly 'empoisoned' his seeing, for Hero becomes to Claudio what he thinks he sees.

There are two kinds of 'seeming truths' at work here. On the one hand, there is the appearance which looks like reality to the eye, and is believed by the mind; on the other, there is psychological truth, that that which the mind believes can direct the eye to see accordingly. Claudio and Don Pedro's minds, thus manipulated by Don John, are predisposed to see Hero in a way that quite contradicts their first impressions. Beatrice and Benedick also see what they believe, once their minds have been played on by hearsay – a fact which is beautifully demonstrated by Benedick's eager discovery of signs of love in Beatrice at the end of

II. 3, in the face of her continued animosity, and so soon after his exaggerated pleas to avoid her company. We are shown the whole process of rationalisation as Benedick modulates from one attitude to another, culminating in his absurd determination to find love in Beatrice's behaviour, while she so clearly remains 'the infernal Ate in good apparel'.

The rapid change in Benedick, however, is not simply for our amusement, nor for the ironic perspective in which it places him by making him, as he has said of Claudio, the 'argument of his own scorn'. His credulity is a neat forerunner to Claudio's and Don Pedro's; but the main point is that there is no real difference between their assumption of Hero's guilt, and his assumption of Beatrice's love (or, for that matter, hers of his at III. 1). The outcome is the factor which shapes or mis-shapes our judgements, just as it has done with the initiation of 'practices'; for when the intentions are good and the result happy, both 'practice' and assumption can evade question.

There has to be a halt called to all this credulity before any happy resolutions are possible, and it is Beatrice who is first to speak out, with her ardent cry at IV. 1.145, 'O, on my soul, my cousin is belied!' This is the truth of what is *known* being asserted against the appearance of what is *noted*; she asserts her faith in Hero. To set things to rights, though, requires a more neutral figure who plans a reinstatement of the truth by working another 'practice' to cure the ill effects of Don John's perverse medicine ('any impediment will be medicinable to me: I am sick in displeasure to him.' II. 2). In giving Hero out for dead, the Friar hopes to promote Claudio's regret, and although he is not shown as specifically regretting his accusations, Claudio is clearly discomfited. At V. 1, both he and Don Pedro are 'high-proof melancholy'. Their treatment of Leonato and Antonio, however, shows no repentance; nor does the disparaging (or is it embarrassed?) reference to the 'old man's daughter'. It takes the initiator of the deception, Borachio, to destroy it and to bring Hero back in favour, just as it has taken Don Pedro to restore things at II. 1; for it is only after Borachio's confession that Claudio comments,

> Sweet Hero, now thy image doth appear
> In the rare semblance that I loved it first.
> (V. 1.252–3)

The wreck caused by Don John's practice, then, is in the end salvaged, but the happier conclusions do not obscure the fact that the plan intended harm, the evil was uncompromising, the result potentially tragic, and the effects keenly felt amongst the characters. The society emerges scathed, and presumably cured of its favourite sport (is that why the Prince is sad at V. 4.123?). All this comes nowhere near the popular image of the world of Shakespearean comedy as sunlit and idyllic. It has been a world placed suddenly at the mercy of its own foolish superficiality.

DOUBLE TONGUES

All the 'practices' on the surface of the plot in fact echo something more fundamental about the society we are watching; there is a duplicity in its rules. The characters, as we have seen, show a culpable level of credulity; they also display themselves as worldly-wise in their witty exchanges. The high value placed on witty talk is not just a matter of social competence, an admired expertise – its very establishment as something to be valued reveals an underlying conflict. Leonato, Hero, Beatrice, Benedick, Margaret, Don Pedro, and Claudio all pun liberally, and at times thoroughly suggestively, but they cannot in that same society, behave with the liberality that their talk might indicate. The contrast between the exchanges and the action reveals this double standard – to be sophisticated and clever is one thing, but to behave as that talk suggests is something else completely. It is a double system of values which potentially threatens them all; the society appears liberal and informal but the reality of its codes is otherwise.

In a sense, Borachio's fabrication about Hero takes its cue from the appearances of the society he observes; it is the logical consequence of the bawdy repartee they all engage in. It is noticeable that such repartee is only acceptable while it remains detached from realities; when the two appear to coincide, everything is suddenly serious and grim. There is suddenly no place for wit (for example, contrast Beatrice and Benedick at II. 1, and at the end of IV. 1). What has happened to all that joking – the constant references to cuckold's horns and unfaithful wives? Or the implication about illegitimacy in Leonato's answer to Don Pedro?

DON PEDRO I think this is your daughter?
LEONATO Her mother hath many times told me so.
(I. 1.102–3)

Or the way that Don Pedro clearly implies his sexual capacities when flirting with Hero ('My visor is Philemon's roof; within the house is Jove'), or enjoys the innuendo of his exchange with Beatrice (II. 1.271ff)? Nearly everyone has partaken of this social game where to make bawdy allusions is an acceptable norm.

But at IV. 1, the light has changed, and sex has become a matter of 'vile encounters'. Leonato recoils, horrified by the shame of the accusations, 'Do not live, Hero, do not ope thine eyes'; and Don Pedro declares stonily,

> I stand dishonoured, that have gone about
> To link my dear friend to a common stale.
>   (IV. 1.63–4)

having flippantly told Benedick (see I. 1.269, and note) that he will 'temporise with the hours'. Their bluff has been well and truly called.

Now, a long tradition in commentary on the play has seen Hero as the innocent, even silent, victim. To interpret her in this way, however, seems to ignore important aspects of her that we are clearly shown. It also creates a considerable problem for comedy, which holds no place for a truly innocent individual who is made to suffer. The point which retains the comic perspective is the fact that the characters 'suffer' in proportion to their follies, and that Hero's follies are the same as everyone else's. She too behaves according to the social norms; she takes part in the worldly level of verbal exchange, she takes part in the deception of Beatrice. As a woman, she conforms with other social codes which Beatrice by contrast exceeds and criticises; but her apparent docility in social gatherings is not an indication of meekness. Alone with Don Pedro (II. 1), or with her women and her cousin (III. 4), she is forthright, determined, competent, and yes, even flirtatious and suggestive. There is a very good reason why so many mistake her behaviour with Don Pedro at the dance – listen to the archness of her tone as she replies to his questions,

DON PEDRO Lady, will you walk about with your
        friend?

HERO So you walk softly, and look sweetly and say
   nothing, I am yours for the walk; and especially
   when I walk away.

DON PEDRO With me in your company?

HERO I may say so, when I please.
      (II. 1.85–91)

She knows how to play her part, thinking that Don Pedro is
courting her; her answers (is this the part Leonato has
rehearsed her for, or one of her own invention?) are
provocative. And when she is asked to assist with the
tricking of Beatrice, she acquiesces with a mock demure-
ness, 'I will do any modest office, my lord, to help my cousin
to a good husband.' (II. 1.368–9)

As Don Pedro has so carefully emphasised (at I. 1.109) she
is her father's daughter; she is also Beatrice's closest friend,
and if we wanted proof of her capabilities, we need only
watch her in full and articulate charge of the snaring of
Beatrice at III. 1. She has learned so well (from Don
Pedro's briefing) that she is as fluent as he in laying the
'false, sweet bait'. The scene of her wedding preparations
(III. 4) provides another image of her, determined in her
opinion about what she will wear, despite Margaret's
advice: 'My cousin's a fool, and thou art another. I'll wear
none but this.' (III. 4.10) She also keeps pace with Margaret's
innuendo without difficulty, commenting ambiguously in
reply,

MARGARET Get you some of this distilled Carduus
   Benedictus and lay it to your heart; it is the only
   thing for a qualm.

HERO There thou prickest her with a thistle.
      (III. 4.71–4)

Neither the tone nor the content of either of these responses could be held as meek innocence.

When she is facing the devastating accusations before the whole congregation, the precise articulation and the tone of her questions can be taken as indication of tightly controlled anger as well as amazement, with a coolly disdainful stress in, 'And seemed I ever as otherwise to you?' and, 'Is my lord well, that he doth speak so wide?'. Her cry, 'True? O God!' seems more of outrage than despair; and she holds out right through the cross-examination, up to the point where Leonato shows that he believes the story ('Hath no man's dagger here a point for me?' IV. 1.108). It is Leonato who defeats her; for it is one thing to be accused by comparative strangers, quite another to be denied by your own father.

As an audience, of course, we are not as surprised as Hero at Leonato's 'infidelity' to her, since we have seen him from the beginning to be a man who adapts readily to all the social environments in which he finds himself – an experienced social chameleon. Whether he is talking elaborately with the Messenger or in greeting Don Pedro, fussing about arrangements for the dance, joking bawdily with his guests, struggling to keep up with the others in the tricking of Benedick, impatient with the constables – no one else is shown playing so many different roles. He is a dweller on the surfaces, quickly convinced and as quickly unconvinced, skating over the depths; the perfect governor of a society which sets a high value on appearances, he responds to what he sees, rather than trusts what he knows.

But that he eventually experiences pain is undeniable, and he becomes gradually more concerned about the injury done to Hero than about the slight to his position. The result is a more steady and solid Leonato. His distress is given major focus at the opening of V. 1 in a scene which treads a difficult path between serious emotion and farcical exaggeration. In taking up the cause so completely, Antonio threatens to confuse sympathies by a drastic over-playing of his part. Yet the audience has to keep in mind that the emotions which generate such reactions are genuine, and this is helped by the bad light in which Claudio and Don Pedro appear, as they try first to avoid Leonato, and then to use the advantages of youthful superiority to cover their uneasiness about the meeting – an uneasiness which is betrayed later in callous references, such as the 'two old men without teeth', and their eagerness to be entertained by Benedick's wit. Their attempt to resurrect witty repartee and innuendo flounders appropriately before Benedick's new seriousness, and by contrast serves to intensify the expressions of horror as they react to Borachio's confession.

FIGHTING TALK

While the content is certainly important in terms of revealing themes such as the duplicity at the heart of the Messinian society, it is by no means the only way in which the characters are revealed to the audience. The way each character plays with language is particularly significant and so too are the metaphors used. The actual exchanges manipulate the surface tones of the play, while the metaphoric themes form pervasive underlying tones; they are also frequently drawn from elements in the context and then used, as metaphors, to elucidate it.

It is easy enough to appreciate the agility of the verbal sparring that occurs throughout the play. Its energy and speed have often been commended, for the prose undeniably leaps into action when Beatrice or Benedick, Claudio, Don Pedro or even Margaret, are in the mood to be 'wit-crackers'. There is a hierarchy in expertise which parallels intellectual rather than social hierarchies; and there are distinctions between those who are conscious of their art, and those who have pretensions to it, but fall short of success.

The great example of the latter is, of course, Dogberry, who exhibits a linguistic pretentiousness, habitually misusing words in his attempts to appear educated. The over-blown quality of his character is amply demonstrated by the way he talks, and in the guise of bringing light-relief to an increasingly serious plot, he is also used by Shakespeare as a central element within it. For it is Dogberry, with all his attempts to proclaim his own importance at the expense of his partner, Verges, and with all his obsequious nonsense (at III. 5), who in fact frustrates the progress of the truth and thus carries responsibility for the anguish caused at IV. 1. The absurdity of his inflated pretensions is also a light example of the corrupting effects of being in authority, and provides Shakespeare with the opportunity of making popular jokes at the expense of the inefficiency of the untrained constables of the Watch: 'We will rather sleep than talk; we know what belongs to a watch.' (III. 3.37–8).

While Dogberry aspires to the standard of exchange set by his superiors, Don John clearly declines to take part in the competition. He makes this plain in the first scene – 'I am not of many words' – and he is distinguished from the society by the mannered solidity of his comments. That he lacks originality is demonstrated as much in this as it is shown by his reliance on a scheme of someone else's invention. He juggles simple associations of words in a euphuistic vein – 'If I can cross him any way, I bless myself everyway', and, 'What life is there in that, to be the death of this marriage' (II. 2.19–20); he does not manipulate ideas. His flattened tone proclaims his melancholy as much as his declared anti-social feeling, and his language generally lacks 'play'. He is as much a misfit linguistically as he is actually. His claim at I. 3, 'I cannot hide what I am', carries a two-fold irony: on the one hand, it is true, for his speech reveals him; but on the other hand, for the purposes of his 'practice' he manages to conceal what he is – his true feeling – quite successfully, though his speech remains awkward,

> You may think I love you not; let that appear
> hereafter, and aim better at me by that I now will
> manifest.
>
> (III. 2.90–2)

By contrast, Borachio has considerable fluency and is much more able to acquit himself; he is also more perceptive about the society, which enables him to frame a trick that will fool it. But he flaws his own scheme by the over-fluency of his inebriated ramblings to Conrade, putting truth into the incompetent hands of the Watch and at the same time commenting (in his remarks about fashion, 'the deformed thief') on a central theme, the discrepancy between appearances and reality ('Thou knowest that the fashion of a doublet, or a hat, or a cloak, is nothing to a man', III. 3.119). The mistake gives rise to his eloquent apology at V. 1, which brings out the full irony:

> I have deceived even your very eyes. What your
> wisdoms could not discover, these shallow fools
> have brought to light.

With those for whom word-play is an accepted norm of social exchange, there is a constant ripple of sexual suggestiveness. This is not only, as we have seen, a question of social point-scoring; it also indicates the covert concerns of the characters and contributes to a revelation of their inconsistencies. It is also often used by Shakespeare to provide other kinds of information. In the first scene, for instance, it offers useful background details: Leonato gives us an insight into Benedick's reputation; Benedick's inability to take Claudio's love seriously denotes their customary attitudes. Various references couched in wit throughout the play indicate an earlier relationship between Beatrice and Benedick, which makes sense of their current animosity – as, for instance, in her reply to Don Pedro telling her that she has lost Benedick's heart:

> Indeed, my lord, he lent it me a while, and I gave him
> use for it, a double heart for his single one. Marry,
> once before he won it of me with false dice;
> therefore your grace may well say I have lost it.
>
> (II. 1.273–6)

The exchanges also provide revealing psychological 'clues' to the characters, as in the repeated emphasis on Benedick's fear of the cuckold's horns and the teasing he incurs for this; or in Beatrice's own determination to let no 'clod of wayward marl' get the better of her.

These two would inevitably be the best graduates of any 'college of wit-crackers', but their witty sparring is a means of evasion, a mask to hide the realities of their feeling from each other and, more importantly, from themselves. It is one of the central ironies of the play that these two who are so assured of their clear-sightedness are in fact blind about themselves. Overall, the range of Beatrice's wit outstrips

Benedick's. Her sorties leave few untouched. Under the guise of speaking 'all mirth and no matter' she has the freedom of an 'all-licensed fool', reducing aspirations and pretensions, or commenting critically on conventions. Even the highest in rank, Don Pedro, becomes a target, put firmly in his place for suggesting that he might marry Beatrice himself (II. 1). In the course of the same scene, she parries Leonato's suggestions that she will be unmarriageable; counter-attacks by highlighting the male bias of the society; warns Hero of the follies of marriage, in her superb adaptation of the dance metaphor; analyses the source of Claudio's 'sickness'. In everything other than her relationship with Benedick, she deals in realities rather than appearances. She can even see her own position in society objectively, as in the subtle observation that she is 'sunburnt' – a metaphor for the unattractiveness of her attitudes in a biased society. For while the affected language of the court inflates people – for example, the Messenger's description of Claudio at I. 1 – her wit cuts them down to size; under her tongue the incomparable soldier becomes a lovesick boy. And in the atmosphere of masculine dominance, her independent mind works acts of sabotage.

Beatrice's independence, then, is being used to focus the assumptions on which the social codes rely; and the metaphors of the play constantly endorse this image, drawn as they are from its male concerns – combat, actual or formalised as fencing, archery, jousting; hunting, snaring and fishing; financial practices, such as usury, loans and accounts – their behaviour is depicted through metaphors drawn from all these activities. It is thus entirely appropriate at the points in the play where seriousness becomes inescapable, where the accepted codes begin to break down, that these metaphors turn into a potentially destructive reality. Benedick has complained that Beatrice 'speaks poniards, and every word stabs' (II. 1.244); Leonato asks, 'Hath no man's dagger here a point for me?' (IV. 1.108). Benedick's wit becomes the sword of his challenge to Claudio:

> CLAUDIO Wilt thou use thy wit?
> BENEDICK It is in my scabbard; shall I draw it?
>
> (V. 1.124–5)

Beatrice wittily alludes to emotional usury (II. 1.274); the 'dear account' that Claudio owes Benedick is his life (IV. 1.334).

HONOURABLE DEFEATS

Many assessments of the play, having made Hero the 'innocent victim', hold Claudio to be 'callous', but this would seem to be taking them both out of their dramatic context. Claudio's behaviour makes sense within the codes the society operates and ironically it is all a matter of what is considered to be honourable behaviour. At the beginning of the play, he turns to the role of lover once he has triumphed in his career as a soldier. His excellence is prominently the topic of the first exchange, between Leonato and the Messenger. At the end of that scene, and now that he has time to feel, he articulates his realisation of love with fine words. His life may have a compartmentalised quality, but the same codes of behaviour pervade both parts of it, and once again he aspires to excellence.

His first venture uses Don Pedro as an agent, and when this appears to fail, he is ready for an immediate retreat from the courtship, with little more injured than his temper. His rapid dismissal is only callous if his love can be considered as something more than the social arrangement that it so obviously is. His 'Farewell therefore, Hero' is, if grudgingly, the practical solution of a soldier losing a fight, and not in any way a romantic cry of pain. But once that muddle is straightened, he allows himself to enter the part of the lover more fully. Benedick's scorn of him at II. 3 is carefully informative; Shakespeare is telling us that Claudio is a perfectionist in this role too. No aspect is left unpolished as he 'dedicates his behaviours to love'. He adopts all the appearances of love that are fashionable, and Hero presumably accepts him at this surface level.

But with appearances those appearances are destroyed. Claudio, like Hero, is society's victim as well as its product. He obeys all the rules, only to discover through Don John that his object seems worthless; Hero does not seem to merit his perfections. From his viewpoint, this is a terrible blow, and as his love is based on what he has noted ('Benedick, didst thou note the daughter of Signor Leonato?' I. 1.158) rather than what he knows, he has no means of defence against the calumny. His behaviours, so carefully trained, have by this time convinced him of his love; he believes in the reality they have created, so what can he do? He reverts with perfect consistency to the fighting codes and seeks revenge for the wound.

His strategy is very swiftly conceived; endorsed by Don Pedro ('And as I wooed for thee to obtain her, I will join with thee to disgrace her'. III. 2) and executed at the church with tactical precision. His exposé follows the process of delusion that he thinks he has experienced; he invites the congregation to appreciate what it sees in Hero, before he indicts her:

Comes not that blood as modest evidence

> To witness simple virtue? Would you not
>   swear
> All you that see her, that she were a maid
> By these exterior shows? But she is none.
>
>   (IV. 1.36–9)

With equal consistency, though, it is a matter of honour to make quick restitution for what he has unwittingly done. Committing himself entirely to Leonato's will – 'dispose/For henceforth of poor Claudio' – he is submitting in military terms. And in this environment, in this society, he is indeed 'poor Claudio'. His resentments and irritations, if not particularly pleasant, have a youthful honesty about them; he is not a villain. It is simply that his whole approach to love by appearances, which has had the approval of his social peers, is a method which through him has been tested by its own devices and found wanting.

Between Beatrice and Benedick the situation is in reverse, for while they appear to be enemies, their love has an underlying reality, even though they both deceive themselves about it. It takes another deception – Don Pedro's 'practice' – to break through this self-deception. On realisation that each is loved by the other, and loves in return, there is a comical, momentary adherence to love as the society plays it – a matter of female subservience on the one hand,

> And, Benedick, love on, I will requite thee
> Taming my wild heart to thy loving hand.
>
>   (III. 1.111–12)

and conventional activities on the other, with Benedick rushing to 'get her picture' (II. 3.264). They both show signs of dedicating their behaviours to love, but the realism with which they see things will not allow this to last; the superficiality of love by conventions is not for those who know each other so well already. Nor is the situation conducive to romantic entertainments; all the surfaces are cut through by Beatrice's dramatic demand that Benedick 'Kill Claudio' (IV. 1.289).

What Beatrice is asking for is not simply a revenge. Her demand is, in effect, for the establishment of new priorities; she wants Benedick to set his love for her above the codes of loyalty to which he has always adhered.

BENEDICK . . . By this hand, I love thee.
BEATRICE Use it for my love some other way than
swearing by it.

(IV. 1.325–8)

The 'practice' which set out to bring them into line with the social conventions never anticipated a result which would in fact make drastic changes to central codes of honour. Benedick's compliance with the demand makes his commitment to Beatrice totally serious. All that remains is for some public bridge to be made between their former animosity and their realised loves, and ironically it is the half-written sonnets, the relics of their attempts to play the game 'properly', which act as this bridge. In the last minute hesitation, these sonnets can be produced as 'evidence'; their final acceptance of each other is determinedly anti-romantic, resorting to their old tones:

BENEDICK Come, I will have thee; but by this light I
take thee for pity.
BEATRICE I would not deny you; but, by this good day
I yield upon great persuasion.

(V. 4.92–5)

The link between their stringent realism and their privately acknowledged love can be made ; even with the knowledge that it can be 'a Scotch jig, a measure, and a cinquepace', love can be found acceptable – 'for man is a giddy thing' (V. 4.109).

Under the Friar's guidance another change is effected, in Leonato's rejection of any serious revenge for the wrong that he and Hero have suffered. He has come a long way, from, 'Hence from her – let her die !' (IV. 1.153) to, 'My soul doth tell me Hero is belied' (V. 1.42). Despite Antonio's advice, 'Make those that do offend you suffer too' (V. 1.40), the wound is not going to be salved in the way that Claudio's has been. The cycle of revenge is broken, and the giving back of Hero to Claudio is an optimistic and forgiving symbol, not so much turning the other cheek as recognising that in some way they are all responsible. The deferment of Benedick's 'brave punishments' for Don John until after the weddings is also important; the comic mode dictates celebration, not retribution.

The values seen emerging at the end of the play, then, seem to be replacing the old codes with more generous, honest and humane rules. They are rules which can only be operated in a society where trust and proper self-knowledge exist; where allegiances are to truth and not to patterns of behaviour; where the game of 'practice' is not played; where things are not destroyed but preserved and enhanced; where things are not 'noted' but known. And as such, they are the rules which are the predominant achievement of comedy, in Messina or elsewhere.

A NOTE ON THE TEXT AND THE DATE OF THE PLAY . . .

The play was first set up in print in 1600, and in August appeared on the Stationer's Register together with *Henry IV, Part 2*, in the edition known as the Quarto. It was not published again until the First Folio edition of 1623, which contains a few minor changes, some corrective, others accidental. The division into acts was not made until the Folio edition.

The Quarto was carefully printed and is believed to have been set from Shakespeare's own manuscript; apart from certain inconsistencies in speech prefixes and entrances, it contains few errors. The present edition is based mainly on the first Quarto with certain emendations of inconsistencies, mainly from the First Folio.

The actual date of the first performance is not known, but the frontispiece of the Quarto makes it clear that the play had already 'been sundry times publicly acted' by Shakespeare's own company of actors, the Chamberlain's men, who from 1599 were able to perform in their own theatre, the first Globe playhouse on Bankside.

. . . AND A NOTE ON THE NOTES

The aim of these has been to avoid what Aldous Huxley (*Proper Studies*, 1927) called 'a horrid little school edition' which rendered a play 'meaningless and dull', and to encourage a 'dramatic' reading of the play – with what J. R. Mulryne calls the 'visualising imagination'.

SUGGESTIONS FOR FURTHER READING

GENERAL

J. R. Mulryne, *Shakespeare: Much Ado About Nothing* Studies in English Literature, no. 16, Arnold

Laurence Lerner, ed., *Shakespeare's Comedies: An Anthology of Modern Criticism* Penguin Shakespeare Library

John Russell Brown, *Shakespeare and his Comedies* Methuen (University paperback)

John Russell Brown (ed.) *Much Ado About Nothing and As You Like It* Casebook Series, Macmillan

R. A. Foakes, ed., *Much Ado About Nothing* (Introduction to), New Penguin Shakespeare

ON SOURCE MATERIAL

Geoffrey Bullough, *Narrative and Dramatic Sources of Shakespeare* (Vol. 2), Routledge and Kegan Paul

Kenneth Muir, *Shakespeare's Sources* (Vol. 1), Methuen

MUCH ADO ABOUT NOTHING

THE CHARACTERS

DON PEDRO, Prince of Arragon

CLAUDIO, of Florence ⎫
⎬ young lords accompanying
BENEDICK, of Padua ⎭ Don Pedro

DON JOHN, Don Pedro's illegitimate brother (sometimes
    called the Bastard)

BORACHIO ⎫
⎬ followers of Don John
CONRADE ⎭

LEONATO, Governor of Messina
ANTONIO, his elderly brother
HERO, Leonato's daughter

MARGARET ⎫
⎬ attendants on Hero
URSULA ⎭

BEATRICE, Leonato's niece, an orphan

BALTHASAR, a singer
FRIAR FRANCIS, a priest

DOGBERRY, the Constable in charge of the Watch
VERGES, the Headborough, Dogberry's partner
A Sexton and several Watchmen
A Boy, servant to Benedick
Antonio's son, Musicians and Attendants of Leonato's
    Household
Other lords attending on Don Pedro, Messengers

ACT ONE, scene 1

Messina. *At the time the play is set, Sicily is under Spanish rule, with the court held at the sea-port of Messina. The play takes place in and around the Governor's house. In this scene, which has four distinct phases, all the main characters are introduced and their relationships to one another established. It takes place outside Leonato's house.*

MESSENGER   *A person of the court rather than a servant.*

[3] by this   *by this time*

[4] leagues   *A rather vague measurement in Shakespeare.*

[5] gentlemen   *He is inquiring about people of rank.*

[6] action   *battle, campaign*

[7] sort   *rank*

name   *social distinction*

[8] A victory . . . itself   *winning is twice as satisfactory*

[9] I find here   *Leonato is still reading the letter.*

[12–13] equally remembered   *rewarded in like proportion*

[13–17] He hath . . . how   *All a very elaborate way of saying that Claudio has excelled himself for one so young — so much so that the Messenger pretends to be lost for words.*

[15–16] better bettered expectation   *i.e. more richly exceeded what could be expected*

[18] an uncle   *He is nowhere else mentioned in the play.*

[21–2] joy . . . enough   *i.e. could not be kept quietly under control*

[22] modest   *moderate*

[23] a badge of bitterness   *i.e. weeping; badge, a sign displayed, is a metaphorical development from* show

[26–9] A kind . . . weeping   *Leonato responds with similar elaboration, punning on* kind *(natural) and* kindness, *ending with a platitude. Their whole exchange is conducted with an exaggerated formality which is quickly dispersed when Beatrice starts to speak.*

ACT ONE

Scene 1. *Enter* LEONATO, HERO *and* BEATRICE, *with a* MESSENGER

LEONATO I learn in this letter that Don Pedro of Arragon comes this night to Messina.

MESSENGER He is very near by this; he was not three leagues off when I left him.

LEONATO How many gentlemen have you lost in this action?

MESSENGER But few of any sort, and none of name.

LEONATO A victory is twice itself when the achiever brings home full numbers. I find here that Don Pedro hath bestowed much honour on a young 10 Florentine called Claudio.

MESSENGER Much deserved on his part, and equally remembered by Don Pedro. He hath borne himself beyond the promise of his age, doing in the figure of a lamb the feats of a lion; he hath indeed better bettered expectation than you must expect of me to tell you how.

LEONATO He hath an uncle here in Messina will be very much glad of it.

MESSENGER I have already delivered him letters, and 20 there appears much joy in him, even so much that joy could not show itself modest enough without a badge of bitterness.

LEONATO Did he break out into tears?

MESSENGER In great measure.

LEONATO A kind overflow of kindness; there are no faces truer than those that are so washed. How

[30] Signor Mountanto   *An ironical name for Benedick. A mountanto was a fencing thrust, and a suitable name for Benedick with whom Beatrice fights verbally.*

[33] sort   *rank*

[36] pleasant   *light-hearted*

[38] set up his bills   *posted notices; Beatrice now gives an example of his light-heartedness.*

[39] at the flight   *to an archery contest*

[39–41] my uncle's ... birdbolt   *the court fool replied on Cupid's behalf, and chose to meet the challenge with the birdbolt. This was the simplest level of archery, using blunt arrows – the only weapons that fools were allowed. The implication is that Benedick also is a fool.*

[41–4] I pray ... killing   *Beatrice is being scornful about Benedick's courage on the battlefield; she has promised to eat all those he kills, on the assumption that he won't kill anyone!*

[45] tax   *deride*

[46] be meet with you   *get even with you (with a pun on* meet/meat, *referring back to the eating)*

[49] holp   *helped. She's suggesting that his good service has been to finish off old provisions (*musty victual*).*

[50] valiant trencher-man   *a great eater. She deliberately uses* valiant *in connection with eating rather than fighting, to belittle Benedick still further.*

[51] stomach   *To the Elizabethans this would suggest more than simply eating food, since the passions were considered to be 'appetites'.*

[53] to a lady   *Beatrice twists the Messenger's reply to mean (1) compared with a lady, (2) in his treatment of women (implying that he is better as a womaniser than on the battlefield).*

[55] stuffed   *filled*

[57–8] stuffed man   *Beatrice implies that Benedick is a dummy. It also refers back to the metaphors of* eating *and* stomach, *with sexual undertones.*

[59] mistake   *misjudge (The Messenger has been taking Beatrice too seriously.)*

[59–62] There ... them   *Leonato explains their relationship, adapting military terms to illustrate their kind of encounters.*

much better is it to weep at joy than to joy at
weeping!

BEATRICE I pray you, is Signor Mountanto returned 30
from the wars, or no?

MESSENGER I know none of that name, lady; there
was none such in the army of any sort.

LEONATO What is he that you ask for, niece?

HERO My cousin means Signor Benedick of Padua.

MESSENGER O, he's returned, and as pleasant as ever
he was.

BEATRICE He set up his bills here in Messina and
challenged Cupid at the flight; and my uncle's fool,
reading the challenge, subscribed for Cupid and 40
challenged him at the birdbolt. I pray you, how
many hath he killed and eaten in these wars? But
how many hath he killed? For indeed, I promised to
eat all of his killing.

LEONATO 'Faith, niece, you tax Signor Benedick too
much; but he'll be meet with you, I doubt it not.

MESSENGER He hath done good service, lady, in these
wars.

BEATRICE You had musty victual, and he hath holp to
eat it; he is a very valiant trencher-man, he hath an 50
excellent stomach.

MESSENGER And a good soldier too, lady.

BEATRICE And a good soldier to a lady. But what is he
to a lord?

MESSENGER A lord to a lord, a man to a man, stuffed
with all honourable virtues.

BEATRICE It is so indeed; he is no less than a stuffed
man. But for the stuffing – well, we are all mortal.

LEONATO You must not, sir, mistake my niece. There
is a kind of merry war betwixt Signor Benedick and 60

[63] gets   *achieves*

[63-4] In . . . off   *Beatrice retains the metaphor, with the image of Benedick's wits limping away as a result of their last verbal encounter.*
halting: *limping*

[64-9] and now . . . creature   *He has, she says, only one of his mental faculties left, which will just about distinguish him as human as opposed to animal. The Elizabethans were much concerned with such delineations.*

[66] wit . . . warm   *A common phrase meaning 'Sufficient sense to keep out the cold'.*

[67] bear it for a difference   *keep it to show the distinction; from heraldry, in which a coat of arms was altered to denote a particular member of a family.*

[69] reasonable creature   *one possessed with the faculty of reason*

[69-70] Who . . . now   *One of several inquiries which clearly show her interest in him.*

[70-1] sworn brother   *a close friend, sworn to loyalty by oath. Not a relationship entered into lightly, so* every month *is again derogatory.*

[73-5] He wears . . . block   *i.e. he's as fickle about his friendships as the changing fashions (for further references to fashion, see III.2.36 and III.3.119).*

[75] block   *wooden mould on which hats are shaped*

[77] books   *favour*

[78] an   *if*

[80] squarer   *brawler (certainly not the kind of companion a young lord should have)*

[85] pestilence   *bubonic plague. A common disease in Elizabethan England, it often caused theatres to be closed.*

[86] the taker . . . mad   *the one who catches it immediately goes mad*

[87] the Benedick   *Beatrice turns his name into that of a disease.*

[88] 'a   *he*

[89] hold   *stay (because she'd be a dangerous enemy!)*

[91] run mad   *i.e. catch the Benedick (by falling in love)*

[93] is approached   *has arrived*

her; they never meet but there's a skirmish of wit
between them.

BEATRICE Alas, he gets nothing by that. In our last
conflict four of his five wits went halting off, and
now is the whole man governed with one; so that if
he have wit enough to keep himself warm, let him
bear it for a difference between himself and his
horse – for it is all the wealth that he hath left, to be
known a reasonable creature. Who is his companion now? He hath every month a new sworn   70
brother.

MESSENGER Is't possible?

BEATRICE Very easily possible. He wears his faith but
as the fashion of his hat; it ever changes with the
next block.

MESSENGER I see, lady, the gentleman is not in your
books.

BEATRICE No; an he were, I would burn my study.
But I pray you, who is his companion? Is there no
young squarer now that will make a voyage with   80
him to the devil?

MESSENGER He is most in the company of the right
noble Claudio.

BEATRICE O Lord, he will hang upon him like a
disease. He is sooner caught than the pestilence,
and the taker runs presently mad. God help the
noble Claudio! If he have caught the Benedick, it
will cost him a thousand pound ere 'a be cured.

MESSENGER I will hold friends with you, lady.

BEATRICE Do, good friend.   90

LEONATO You will never run mad, niece.

BEATRICE No, not till a hot January.

MESSENGER Don Pedro is approached.

[Flourish. Enter] *The second phase of the scene now begins. Although only main characters are named, Don Pedro would certainly be accompanied by other attendants. The conventions of greeting are observed and wit is soon established as socially acceptable.*

[94] are you come *(this seems to indicate Leonato's movement across the stage)*

[95–6] The fashion . . . it *it's more usual for people to avoid trouble than to go out of their way to meet it*

[96] cost *(1) trouble (2) expense*
encounter *come to meet*

[97–100] Never . . . leave *Leonato is flattering Don Pedro in return, saying that trouble comes when he leaves rather than when he arrives – dramatic irony in view of what happens during this particular visit.*

[101] charge *(1) responsibilities (2) expense*

[103] Her . . . so *His indirect reply must be intended to incite a witty response, showing a more informal atmosphere replacing the elaboration of greeting.*

[105–6] for then were you a child *He is quick to stab back, suggesting that there was no threat to women before Benedick was sexually mature.*

[107] You have it full *you're well answered*

[107–8] we . . . are *now we know what sort of reputation you have*

[109] fathers herself *shows who her father is, because she looks like him*

[109–10] for . . . father *the father you resemble is much respected*

[112] his head *i.e. with his white hair and beard*

[113] as like him as she is *however like him she is*

[114] still *always*

[115] nobody marks you *no one's listening to you; also implicit stage direction: the other characters continue to talk to each other, leaving Benedick and Beatrice central for their first full exchange.*

[116] Lady Disdain *The personification of an attribute, like this and (Lady) Courtesy, was a common convention in literature.*

yet *still*

[119] meet *suitable (and a pun – meat)*

[120–1] Courtesy . . . presence *when you're around even the best of manners can't help but change to scorn*

[123–4] And I . . . heart *I wish I could find it in me to love them. The first heart means inmost being, and the second, feelings.*

Flourish. Enter DON PEDRO, CLAUDIO, BENEDICK, BALTHASAR
  and DON JOHN

DON PEDRO Good Signor Leonato, are you come to
  meet your trouble? The fashion of the world is to
  avoid cost, and you encounter it.

LEONATO Never came trouble to my house in the
  likeness of your grace. For trouble being gone,
  comfort should remain; but when you depart from
  me, sorrow abides and happiness takes his leave.   100

DON PEDRO You embrace your charge too willingly. I
  think this is your daughter?

LEONATO Her mother hath many times told me so.

BENEDICK Were you in doubt, sir, that you asked her?

LEONATO Signor Benedick, no, for then were you a
  child.

DON PEDRO You have it full, Benedick; we may guess
  by this what you are, being a man. Truly, the lady
  fathers herself. Be happy, lady, for you are like an
  honourable father. [*He begins to talk aside to Leonato*] 110

BENEDICK If Signor Leonato be her father, she would
  not have his head on her shoulders for all Messina,
  as like him as she is.

BEATRICE I wonder that you will still be talking,
  Signor Benedick; nobody marks you.

BENEDICK What, my dear Lady Disdain, are you yet
  living?

BEATRICE Is it possible disdain should die, while she
  hath such meet food to feed it as Signor Benedick?
  Courtesy itself must convert to disdain, if you come 120
  in her presence.

BENEDICK Then is courtesy a turncoat; but it is certain
  I am loved of all ladies, only you excepted. And I
  would I could find in my heart that I had not a hard

39

[127] pernicious *wicked*

[128] and my cold blood *She, like Benedick, seems anxious to assert that she is not given to emotional response.*

I am of your humour *I'm of the same temperament. The humours were thought to be substances in the body, which, by different combinations, determined a person's character (a medieval theory).*

[129–30] I had . . . me *She is even more emphatic about her 'hard heart' than Benedick.*

[132–3] a predestinate scratched face *i.e. the inevitable outcome of a relationship with her (implying her bad temper)*

[135] an 'twere *if it were*

[136] a rare parrot-teacher *an excellent parrot teacher (you're so good at talking to no purpose)*

[137–8] A bird . . . yours *better a bird speaking my language than a beast speaking yours. Compare l. 67.*

[139] would *wish*

[140] a continuer *at keeping going* keep your way *carry on*

[141] a' *in (derived from a corruption of 'of')* done *finished*

[142] a jade's trick *A jade is a bad horse, which might stop suddenly and throw its rider; Benedick withdraws from the 'skirmish', and Beatrice, it seems, now sees no difference between him and his horse. (See l. 67 ff.)*

[142–3] I know you of old *A neat way of indicating their long-standing contact, confirming what we have been told earlier in the scene.*

[144] the sum of all *how things are (The tail-end of their conversation; he then turns to address everyone again.)*

[148] some occasion may detain *something may happen to detain (dramatic irony again)*

[150–1] you shall not be forsworn *you won't be disappointed (literally: you won't have sworn falsely)*

[152] being reconciled *since you are now reconciled. This is the first indication of the tension between the brothers which is soon to take on more importance in the plot.*

[153] I owe you all duty *I am entirely at your service*

[154–5] I thank . . . you *His curt response contrasts baldly with the elaborate politeness and social ease of the other speakers.*

[156] Please it *will it please*

[157] we will go together *Don Pedro won't take formal precedence but maintains the friendly atmosphere.*

heart, for truly I love none.

BEATRICE A dear happiness to women; they would else have been troubled with a pernicious suitor! I thank God and my cold blood, I am of your humour for that; I had rather hear my dog bark at a crow than a man swear he loves me. 130

BENEDICK God keep your ladyship still in that mind so some gentleman or other shall 'scape a predestinate scratched face!

BEATRICE Scratching could not make it worse, an 'twere such a face as yours were.

BENEDICK Well, you are a rare parrot-teacher.

BEATRICE A bird of my tongue is better than a beast of yours.

BENEDICK I would my horse had the speed of your tongue, and so good a continuer. But keep your way 140 a' God's name, I have done.

BEATRICE You always end with a jade's trick; I know you of old.

DON PEDRO That is the sum of all, Leonato. [*Aloud*] Signor Claudio and Signor Benedick, my dear friend Leonato hath invited you all. I tell him we shall stay here at the least a month, and he heartily prays some occasion may detain us longer. I dare swear he is no hypocrite, but prays from his heart.

LEONATO If you swear, my lord, you shall not be 150 forsworn. [*To* DON JOHN] Let me bid you welcome, my lord – being reconciled to the Prince your brother, I owe you all duty.

DON JOHN I thank you. I am not of many words, but I thank you.

LEONATO Please it your grace lead on?

DON PEDRO Your hand, Leonato; we will go together.

[158] note   *observe; a crucial verb in the play as* nothing *was pronounced the same as* noting. *It also provides some stage direction for Claudio during the foregoing exchanges. (The third phase begins here.)*

[160] I noted . . . her   *I saw her, but I took no particular notice*

[161] modest   *demure; also implying 'pure' – an important consideration to Claudio.*

[162–5] Do . . . sex?   *Benedick is asking what kind of an answer Claudio wants, and so reveals his awareness that he plays a role (*my custom*) in being a tyrant to women.*

[162] honest   *(1) respectable (2) chaste (linking it to the second sense of* modest *– Benedick is teasing him again)*

[163] simple   *unaffected* [164] after my custom   *as I usually do*

[167–8] Why . . . praise   *Despite Claudio's desire for a serious opinion, Benedick remains light.*   too low   *not tall enough*

[169–71] Only. . .unhandsome   *I can only praise her on one count: if she were different she wouldn't be pretty (a very grudging compliment)*

[173] in sport   *joking; Claudio's use of* thou *and* thee *shows quite clearly that he is imparting confidential information to his friend in all seriousness. Benedick's constant use of 'you' until l. 196, shows that he is not taking Claudio at all seriously until that point.*

[177] Can . . . jewel   *Claudio is implying that all the wealth in the world would not equal her value.*

[178] and a case   *Still flippant, Benedick suggests the jewel is easily purchased, case and all. There is a bawdy joke at work here as well.*

[178–79] But . . . brow   *Benedick still can't decide whether Claudio is serious.* sad brow: *serious expression*

[179–80] play the flouting Jack   *play the knave (who deceives someone into believing something that isn't true, in order to laugh at him)*

[180] to tell us   *i.e. expecting us to believe*

[180–1] Cupid . . . carpenter   *Cupid was proverbially blind, in order to strike hearts by chance, and hence couldn't possibly catch a fast-moving hare; Vulcan, a Roman god, was a blacksmith.*

[181–2] Come . . . song   *Again, he tries to find out whether Claudio is fooling him or not, this time with a musical metaphor;* go in   *join in*

[185] spectacles   *These were first worn in the fifteenth century.*

[186] no such matter   *nothing of the kind*   an   *if*

[187] with a fury   *(1) a bad temper (2) a reference to mythological beings, the Furies, whose task it was to exact vengeance.*

exceeds her as much in beauty   *Beatrice has impressed him!*

[Exeunt all but BENEDICK *and* CLAUDIO

CLAUDIO Benedick, didst thou note the daughter of
Signor Leonato?

BENEDICK I noted her not, but I looked on her.   160

CLAUDIO Is she not a modest young lady?

BENEDICK Do you question me as an honest man
should do, for my simple true judgement? Or would
you have me speak after my custom, as being a
professed tyrant to their sex?

CLAUDIO No, I pray thee speak in sober judgement.

BENEDICK Why, i' faith, methinks she's too low for a
high praise, too brown for a fair praise, and too little
for a great praise. Only this commendation I can
afford her – that were she other than she is, she were 170
unhandsome; and being no other but as she is, I do
not like her.

CLAUDIO Thou thinkest I am in sport. I pray thee tell
me truly how thou likest her.

BENEDICK Would you buy her, that you inquire after
her?

CLAUDIO Can the world buy such a jewel?

BENEDICK Yea, and a case to put it into. But speak you
this with a sad brow? Or do you play the flouting
Jack, to tell us Cupid is a good hare-finder, and 180
Vulcan a rare carpenter? Come, in what key shall a
man take you to go in the song?

CLAUDIO In mine eye she is the sweetest lady that ever
I looked on.

BENEDICK I can see yet without spectacles, and I see
no such matter. There's her cousin, an she were not
possessed with a fury, exceeds her as much in beauty
as the first of May doth the last of December. But I
hope you have no intent to turn husband, have
you?   190

43

[193–5] In faith ... suspicion   *i.e. isn't there anyone left who doesn't want to run the risk of being thought a cuckold; Benedick's tone is incredulous since he equates being married with being made a cuckold (the name for a man with an unfaithful wife).*

[194–5] wear ... suspicion   *Proverbially a cap was worn to cover the horns which were the mark of the cuckold, and as such a symbol of ridicule.*

[195] threescore   *sixty*

[196] Go to   *an expression of disbelief (compare 'Get away with you!')*   An thou wilt needs   *if you must*

[197] wear the print of it   *carry the mark made by it (i.e. bear the consequences, one of which might be a set of horns)*

[197–8] sigh away Sundays   *(1) as a married man, Sunday will no longer be a free day, or (2) you'll never be able to relax (wondering what your wife is up to)*

[201] followed not   *did not come with us*

[202] constrain me   *make me*

[204] on thy allegiance   *on the loyalty that you owe me*

[205–8] I can ... love   *Benedick continues to joke: he could keep a secret, he says, but now he has no choice since he has been asked on his allegiance (a condition he has invited with his use of* constrain *at l. 202)*

[208–9] that is your grace's part   *that should have been your line*

[211] If ... uttered   *if it's true that I am in love then this would be the right answer*

[212] the old tale   *the same old story. The actual story referred to is uncertain, but the general sense is that the emphatic denials (*It is not so, nor 'twas not so*) are undercut by the last part, which suggests it might well become so.*

[214–15] God forbid it should be otherwise   *Claudio brings his feeling into the open.*

[216] Amen   *so be it. A suitable rejoinder to Claudio's 'prayer'; Don Pedro finds no difficulty in taking Claudio seriously.*

[218] to fetch me in   *to trick me into honesty*

[219] speak my thought   *say what I'm really thinking*

[221] two faiths and troths   *Benedick is now making fun of both of them, under the guise of swearing by his double commitments. During this speedy exchange, the focus of the scene shifts from Claudio, whose sincerity is taken seriously by Don Pedro, to Benedick, whose levity now comes under scrutiny.*

CLAUDIO I would scarce trust myself, though I had
sworn the contrary, if Hero would be my wife.

BENEDICK Is't come to this? In faith, hath not the
world one man but he will wear his cap with
suspicion? Shall I never see a bachelor of threescore
again? Go to, i' faith! An thou wilt needs thrust thy
neck into a yoke, wear the print of it – and sigh
away Sundays. Look, Don Pedro is returned to seek
you.

Enter DON PEDRO

DON PEDRO What secret hath held you here, that you 200
followed not to Leonato's?

BENEDICK I would your grace would constrain me to
tell.

DON PEDRO I charge thee, on thy allegiance.

BENEDICK You hear, Count Claudio? I can be secret
as a dumb man; I would have you think so. But on
my allegiance – mark you this, on my allegiance –
he is in love. With who? Now that is your grace's
part. Mark how short his answer is – with Hero,
Leonato's short daughter. 210

CLAUDIO If this were so, so were it uttered.

BENEDICK Like the old tale, my lord, 'It is not so, nor
'twas not so; but indeed, God forbid it should be so.'

CLAUDIO If my passion change not shortly, God forbid
it should be otherwise!

DON PEDRO Amen, if you love her, for the lady is very
well worthy.

CLAUDIO You speak this to fetch me in, my lord.

DON PEDRO By my troth, I speak my thought.

CLAUDIO And in faith, my lord, I spoke mine. 220

BENEDICK And by my two faiths and troths, my lord, I

[227] in it   *i.e. convinced of it*

[229] heretic   *Don Pedro picks up Benedick's use of fire and stake.*

[229–30] in the despite of   *in your contempt for (beauty/women)*

[231–2] And . . . will   *Claudio implies that Benedick can only play this role with difficulty, which is strenuously denied.*

[235–7] But . . . me   *More references to the dreaded horns. Benedick's philosophy for remaining single depends on his alleged conviction that all wives are unfaithful.*

[235] recheat   *hunting call*

[236] winded   *blown*

in my forehead   *i.e. where the cuckold's horns were to be found*

bugle   *i.e. penis*

[237] invisible baldrick   *unseen belt (i.e. vagina)*

shall pardon   *must excuse*

[240] fine   *(1) conclusion (2) penalty (for this belief)*

go the finer   *fare better*

[245] Prove that ever I lose   *if you can ever prove that I lose*

[246] get again with drinking   *Wine-drinking was thought to renew the blood (while love wasted it).*

[247] ballad-maker's pen   *Used for writing love poems, and hence a suitable implement!*

[248–9] and hang . . . Cupid   *turn me into a brothel-sign (like a pub sign). For blind Cupid see note on l. 180.*

[250] fall from this faith   *lapse, as from a religion (see back to heretic in line 229, etc.)*

[251] thou . . . argument   *(1) you will become a great topic for discussion (2) you will become a famous example*

[252] hang . . . cat   *A reference to the use of a cat, hung in a basket, for target practice in archery.*

[254] Adam   *Thought by many editors to refer to a famous archer of the previous century, Adam Bell.*

spoke mine.

CLAUDIO That I love her, I feel.

DON PEDRO That she is worthy, I know.

BENEDICK That I neither feel how she should be loved, nor know how she should be worthy, is the opinion that fire cannot melt out of me; I will die in it at the stake.

DON PEDRO Thou wast ever an obstinate heretic in the despite of beauty. 230

CLAUDIO And never could maintain his part but in the force of his will.

BENEDICK That a woman conceived me, I thank her; that she brought me up, I likewise give her most humble thanks. But that I will have a recheat winded in my forehead, or hang my bugle in an invisible baldrick, all women shall pardon me. Because I will not do them the wrong to mistrust any, I will do myself the right to trust none; and the fine is – for the which I may go the finer – I will live 240 a bachelor.

DON PEDRO I shall see thee, ere I die, look pale with love.

BENEDICK With anger, with sickness, or with hunger, my lord; not with love. Prove that ever I lose more blood with love than I will get again with drinking, pick out mine eyes with a ballad-maker's pen, and hang me up at the door of a brothel-house for the sign of blind Cupid.

DON PEDRO Well, if ever thou dost fall from this faith, 250 thou wilt prove a notable argument.

BENEDICK If I do, hang me in a bottle like a cat and shoot at me; and he that hits me, let him be clapped on the shoulder and called Adam.

[255] as time shall try   *Compare the expression 'Time will tell'.*

[255–6] 'In time . . . yoke'   *i.e. Everything succumbs, given time. A line roughly quoted either from an earlier play –* The Spanish Tragedy, *by Kyd, c. 1587 – or from a sonnet by Thomas Watson.*

[258] it   *i.e. the yoke*

[259] in my forehead   *Back again to the horns of the deceived husband. (Compare l. 197)*   vilely   *crudely*

[260–2] and in . . . sign   *just as they write in big letters for an advertisement to hire a horse, let them put under my picture*

[265] horn-mad   *crazy; a common adjective, here emphasising* horn.

[266–7] if Cupid . . . shortly   *if Cupid has any arrows left after being in Venice, you will be the next to be struck*

[266] quiver   *A case for holding arrows; punning on* quake.

[267] Venice   *Then a rich city, famous for immorality.*

[268] I look for an earthquake too   *if it happens I'll expect a massive disaster (i.e. it's about as unlikely as an earthquake)*

[269] temporise with the hours   *(1) weaken as time goes by (be tempered by it), or (2) give in after a while (*temporise: *yield to circumstance). Also a pun –* hours/whores, *pronounced similarly.*

[270] repair   *make your way.*

[274] matter   *sense. Benedick is being ironical about the simplicity of the task, which he recognises as a means of getting rid of him.*

[275] and so I commit you   *A conventional form of farewell.*

[276] tuition   *protection. Claudio breaks in, continuing with a typical letter-ending.*

[278–9] The sixth . . . Benedick   *Don Pedro finishes 'the letter' off; the date was the old Midsummer Day, implying Midsummer madness.*

[280–2] The body . . . neither   *the main part of your conversation might be trimmed with details, but they are only loosely relevant. He is being scathing about the quality of their verbal wit.*

[281] discourse *conversation*   guarded *ornamented (usually of clothes)*

[282] basted   *stitched loosely*

[283] flout old ends   *mock me (with an allusion to their parody of the letter-ending)*

[283–4] examine your conscience   *i.e. look to yourselves*

[Exit]   *At Benedick's exit the last phase of the scene begins, marked also by the change to blank verse. This reflects the communication of more formal matters, in contrast with the flexibility and speed of witty prose exchange.*

[285] liege   *lord (to whom allegiance is due)*   do me good: *help me*

DON PEDRO Well, as time shall try. 'In time the savage bull doth bear the yoke.'

BENEDICK The savage bull may, but if ever the sensible Benedick bear it, pluck off the bull's horns, and set them in my forehead. And let me be vilely painted, and in such great letters as they write, 260 'Here is good horse to hire,' let them signify under my sign, 'Here you may see Benedick, the married man.'

CLAUDIO If this should ever happen thou wouldst be horn-mad.

DON PEDRO Nay, if Cupid have not spent all his quiver in Venice, thou wilt quake for this shortly.

BENEDICK I look for an earthquake too, then.

DON PEDRO Well, you will temporise with the hours. In the meantime, good Signor Benedick, repair to 270 Leonato's, commend me to him, and tell him I will not fail him at supper; for indeed he hath made great preparation.

BENEDICK I have almost matter enough in me for such an embassage; and so I commit you –

CLAUDIO To the tuition of God. From my house – if I had it –

DON PEDRO The sixth of July. Your loving friend, Benedick.

BENEDICK Nay, mock not, mock not. The body of 280 your discourse is sometime guarded with fragments, and the guards are but slightly basted on neither. Ere you flout old ends any further, examine your conscience; and so I leave you. [*Exit*

CLAUDIO My liege, your highness now may do me good.

DON PEDRO My love is thine to teach; teach it but how,

[287] apt *ready*

[289] Hath Leonato any son *The motivation for this question is not clear. Claudio may be using it as a means of returning to the topic of Hero ; or ascertaining what financial gain marriage to Hero would be.*

[290] she's his only heir *This assumes the second meaning. To an Elizabethan audience this kind of consideration would be perfectly in order.*

[291] affect *love* [292) this ended action *the war just over*

[297] Have left . . . vacant *i.e. have gone*

in their rooms *Again the idea of thoughts 'inhabiting' the mind*

[288] Come thronging *come crowding in. In speech, a beautifully gentle line, to express the awakening of love.*

[289] prompting *reminding* [300] ere *before*

[302] And tire . . . words *and exhaust us with all your outpourings. Traditionally the lover invaded the mistress with poems of adulation, and Don Pedro's direct, practical approach certainly makes Claudio seem wordy.*

[303] cherish it *foster it secretly* [304] break *broach the subject*

[305] And thou shalt have her *He confidently assumes the success of such a venture, and states it with a kind of military certainty.*

[306] twist so fine a story *tell such an elaborate tale.* Twist *and* fine *are both metaphors from spinning : silk thread and wool yarn are refined by constant twisting (compare the expression* 'spin a tale'*). Was't not to this end would seem to suggest that he has impatiently interrupted Claudio.*

[307] How . . . love *Comical in view of Don Pedro's interruption.*

[308] by his complexion *i.e. by the way I look (rather than by hearing full explanations, of the kind Don Pedro is anxious to avoid)*

[309] too sudden seem *might seem to have come about very quickly (and therefore be thought shallow)*

[310] I would . . . treatise *I would have preferred to account for it in greater detail. (1) He wants to demonstrate that his love is genuine; or (2) he wants Hero to be approached more delicately than Don Pedro proposes; or (3) (most of all?) he wants to talk about it himself, and neither Benedick nor Don Pedro has given him the chance!*

[311] What . . . flood *why build a bridge broader than the river you cross; i.e. if the message is clear, why elaborate? Military practicality again.*

[312] The fairest . . . necessity *, the best thing (I can do for you) is see that you get what you want*

[313] Look . . . fit *the best way is the one that brings results (see* II. 1.193) *'tis once briefly*

[314] fit . . . remedy *provide thee a cure (compare* salved, *l. 310)*

And thou shalt see how apt it is to learn
Any hard lesson that may do thee good.

CLAUDIO Hath Leonato any son, my lord?

DON PEDRO No child but Hero, she's his only heir. 290
Dost thou affect her, Claudio?

CLAUDIO   O my lord,
When you went onward on this ended action,
I looked upon her with a soldier's eye,
That liked, but had a rougher task in hand
Than to drive liking to the name of love;
But now I am returned, and that war-thoughts
Have left their places vacant, in their rooms
Come thronging soft and delicate desires,
All prompting me how fair young Hero is,
Saying I liked her ere I went to wars—   300

DON PEDRO Thou wilt be like a lover presently,
And tire the hearer with a book of words.
If thou dost love fair Hero, cherish it,
And I will break with her and with her father,
And thou shalt have her. Was't not to this end
That thou began'st to twist so fine a story?

CLAUDIO How sweetly you do minister to love,
That know love's grief by his complexion!
But lest my liking might too sudden seem,
I would have salved it with a longer treatise. 310

DON PEDRO What need the bridge much broader
than the flood?
The fairest grant is the necessity.
Look what will serve is fit; 'tis once, thou
lovest,
And I will fit thee with the remedy.
I know we shall have revelling tonight.
I will assume thy part in some disguise,

[318] in her bosom   *privately*

unclasp my heart   *Compare the expression 'open my heart to'; unclasp could also refer back to that book of words since books at that time often had clasps.*

[320] And . . . tale   *He expresses his strategy in a soldier's terms (take prisoner, force, strong) which lie in strange juxtaposition with amorous.*

[323] In practice . . . presently   *Don Pedro is for immediate action; this is the first time we see him as instigator of a* practice – *a scheme to manipulate feelings – which is a major occupation in the play.*

ACT ONE, scene 2

A brief scene of preparation for the evening celebrations, this contains the first incidence of hearsay in the play which is, significantly, inaccurate.

[1–2] How . . . music   *We now see the private side of the host, fussing about the details of his arrangements.*

[1] cousin   *kinsman*

[2] your son   *Only mentioned in this scene.*

[5] they   *'News' was a plural noun in the sixteenth century.*

[6] As the event stamps them   *that depends what the outcome is*

[6–7] but . . . outward   *but on the face of it, it certainly looks all right*

[8] thick-pleached alley   *a walk (in the orchard) thickly hedged with interwoven branches*

[10] discovered   *revealed*

[13] accordant   *agreeable*

[13–14] take the present time by the top   *take advantage of the moment (from the proverb 'Take time by the forelock')*

[14] break with you of it   *broach the subject with you*

[15] wit   *intelligence*

[17] and question   *i.e. so that you can question*

[18–19] we . . . itself   *i.e. we'll wait until it happens (though in fact he prepares Hero)*

[21] peradventure   *by any chance*

And tell fair Hero I am Claudio,
And in her bosom I'll unclasp my heart,
And take her hearing prisoner with the force
And strong encounter of my amorous tale.   320
Then after to her father will I break,
And the conclusion is, she shall be thine.
In practice let us put it presently.

                                    [*Exeunt*

Scene 2. *Enter* LEONATO *and* ANTONIO

LEONATO How now, brother? Where is my cousin,
    your son? Hath he provided this music?

ANTONIO He is very busy about it. But, brother, I can
    tell you strange news that you yet dreamt not of.

LEONATO Are they good?

ANTONIO As the event stamps them; but they have a
    good cover, they show well outward. The Prince
    and Count Claudio, walking in a thick-pleached
    alley in mine orchard, were thus much overheard
    by a man of mine: the Prince discovered to Claudio   10
    that he loved my niece your daughter, and meant to
    acknowledge it this night in a dance; and if he
    found her accordant, he meant to take the present
    time by the top and instantly break with you of it.

LEONATO Hath the fellow any wit that told you this?

ANTONIO A good sharp fellow. I will send for him, and
    question him yourself.

LEONATO No, no, we will hold it as a dream till it
    appear itself. But I will acquaint my daughter
    withal, that she may be the better prepared for an   20
    answer, if peradventure this be true. Go you and tell
    her of it.

[23] Cousins   *He addresses them all generally.*

[24] O, I cry you mercy   *I beg your pardon (for including him with the attendants)*

ACT ONE, scene 3

This scene is one of dramatic economy. Information is given and background detail supplied to make clear Don John's motivation.

[1] What the good-year   *A general expletive, like 'What the devil!'*

[2] out of measure   *excessively*

[3–4] There . . . limit   *there is no limit to the reasons which cause my melancholy*

[6–7] what blessing brings it   *what good will it do*

[8] present   *immediate*

[8–9] a patient sufferance   *a means of enduring (from having reasoned it out)*

[11] born under Saturn   *To be born when this planet was dominant astrologically was thought to produce a gloomy character (hence, saturnine).*

goest about to   *attempt to*

[11–12] to apply . . . mischief   *to provide a psychological solution to a deadly physical problem (either his disposition or his illegitimacy)*

[12–13] I cannot hide what I am   *I cannot conceal my true self (though he manages to later on, with terrible result)*

[14–15] when I have stomach   *when I feel like it*

[15] and wait . . . leisure   *i.e. and not wait for anyone else*

[16] tend   *attend*

[17] claw . . . humour   *i.e. placate no man who is moody; claw: scratch in a soothing manner. His whole philosophy adds up to, 'I'll do what I like, when I like, regardless of anyone else'.*

[19] without controlment   *freely*

[19–21] You have . . . grace   *Brief background information, without unnecessary detail.*

[21–4] where . . . harvest   *you will only become secure (in his favour) by virtue of your own efforts; you will have to work to turn things to your advantage*

Enter ATTENDANTS, *led by* ANTONIO'S SON *with*
BALTHASAR

Cousins, you know what you have to do. [*To*
BALTHASAR] O, I cry you mercy, friend; go with me
and I will use your skill. [*To* ANTONIO'S SON] Good
cousin, have a care this busy time.

[*Exeunt*

Scene 3. *Enter* DON JOHN *and* CONRADE *his companion*

CONRADE What the good-year, my lord! Why are you
thus out of measure sad?

DON JOHN There is no measure in the occasion that
breeds; therefore the sadness is without limit.

CONRADE You should hear reason.

DON JOHN And when I have heard it, what blessing
brings it?

CONRADE If not a present remedy, at least a patient
sufferance.

DON JOHN I wonder that thou – being, as thou sayest   10
thou art, born under Saturn – goest about to apply a
moral medicine to a mortifying mischief. I cannot
hide what I am. I must be sad when I have cause,
and smile at no man's jests; eat when I have
stomach, and wait for no man's leisure; sleep when
I am drowsy, and tend on no man's business; laugh
when I am merry, and claw no man in his humour.

CONRADE Yea, but you must not make the full show of
this till you may do it without controlment. You
have of late stood out against your brother, and he   20
hath ta'en you newly into his grace, where it is
impossible you should take true root but by the fair

[24] frame   *engineer*

[25] canker   *the wild or dog-rose (He would rather be independent than in favour.)*

[26] better fits my blood   *(1) is more suitable for my temperament, (2) more suitable because I'm illegitimate*

[27] fashion a carriage   *contrive a way of behaving*

[28–30] though . . . villain   *though no one can accuse me of being deceitfully honest, they will have to concede that I am a straight crook*

[30–1] I . . . clog   *Don John feels himself a captive, neither trusted (hence muzzled, like a dangerous animal) nor free.* clog: *a wooden block attached to the leg, to prevent escape*

[32] decreed   *decided*

not to sing in my cage   *i.e. not to pretend to be happy (or, not to give any pleasure)*

[32–3] had my mouth   *i.e. wasn't muzzled*

[37] I . . . only   *(on the contrary) I use it entirely, for it's the only thing I use (a play on only)*

[42] intelligence   *information; an announcement giving Borachio control of the conversation, which he clearly enjoys.*

[44] model   *framework*

[45] What is he for a fool   *what kind of idiot is he*

[46] unquietness   *anxiety. His assumptions about marriage seem similar to Benedick's.*

[48] most exquisite   *His tone is sarcastic.*

[50] A proper squire   *a fine young lover (again, sarcastic)*

weather that you make yourself; it is needful that
you frame the season for your own harvest.

DON JOHN I had rather be a canker in a hedge than a
rose in his grace, and it better fits my blood to be
disdained of all than to fashion a carriage to rob
love from any. In this, though I cannot be said to be
a flattering honest man, it must not be denied but I
am a plain-dealing villain. I am trusted with a   30
muzzle and enfranchised with a clog – therefore I
have decreed not to sing in my cage. If I had my
mouth, I would bite; if I had my liberty, I would do
my liking. In the meantime, let me be that I am,
and seek not to alter me.

CONRADE Can you make no use of your discontent?

DON JOHN I make all use of it, for I use it only. Who
comes here?

Enter BORACHIO

What news, Borachio?

BORACHIO I came yonder from a great supper. The   40
Prince your brother is royally entertained by
Leonato, and I can give you intelligence of an
intended marriage.

DON JOHN Will it serve for any model to build mischief
on? What is he for a fool that betroths himself to
unquietness?

BORACHIO Marry, it is your brother's right hand.

DON JOHN Who – the most exquisite Claudio?

BORACHIO Even he.

DON JOHN A proper squire! And who? And who?   50
Which way looks he?

[52] one Hero   *i.e. a certain young lady called Hero*

[54] forward March-chick   *i.e. precocious young woman (like a young bird hatched early in the year)*

[54–5] How . . . this   *how did you hear about this*

[56] entertained for   *employed as*

[57] smoking a musty room   *To sweeten the atmosphere – another preparation for the guests; this was done by burning scented wood.*

comes me   *in comes*

[59] arras   *tapestry wall-hanging*

[63–4] This . . . displeasure   *i.e. this may give me something to go on*

[64–5] That . . . overthrow   *This provides a straightforward motivation of jealousy: Claudio has excelled in the military campaign against Don John.*

[65] cross   *thwart; a pun in connection with* bless *since to bless yourself means making the sign of the cross.*

[67] sure   *reliable*

[70] that I am subdued   *(1) now that I've been defeated (2) when my spirits are low*

[70–1] Would the cook were a' my mind   *I wish the cook were of the same mind as myself (i.e. poisonous); rather blackly humorous.*

[71] prove   *test out*

[72] wait upon   *attend*

BORACHIO Marry, one Hero, the daughter and heir of
Leonato.

DON JOHN A very forward March-chick! How came
you to this?

BORACHIO Being entertained for a perfumer, as I was
smoking a musty room, comes me the Prince and
Claudio, hand in hand in sad conference. I
whipped me behind the arras, and there heard it
agreed upon that the Prince should woo Hero for   60
himself, and having obtained her, give her to Count
Claudio.

DON JOHN Come, come, let us thither. This may prove
food to my displeasure. That young start-up hath
all the glory of my overthrow – if I can cross him
any way, I bless myself every way. You are both
sure, and will assist me?

CONRADE To the death, my lord.

DON JOHN Let us to the great supper – their cheer is the
greater that I am subdued. Would the cook were a'   70
my mind! Shall we go prove what's to be done?

BORACHIO We'll wait upon your lordship.

[*Exeunt*

ACT TWO, scene 1

*We now move inside Leonato's house later the same evening; the
'great supper' is over and the masked dance about to begin. The text
cannot convey the visual impact of this; it is an occasion of brilliance
and movement, and also acts as a symbol for underlying issues in the
play. The whole scene, like the dance itself, is a kaleidoscopic
sequence, with characters grouping and re-grouping; at the end there
is the appearance of a settlement and a plan for a new 'practice'.
Like I.1, the scene has distinct phases, each of which marks a
particular progression in plot and character revelation.*

[3] tartly   *sour. Beatrice puns by using the word with* heart-burned,
suggesting his acid flavour.

[5] melancholy   *As one of the four medieval 'humours' (see I.128),
melancholy arose from a predominance of 'black bile' in the body, so Hero
also is punning on* heart-burned.

[6] were   *would be*

[8] image   *picture*

[9] like my lady's eldest son   *i.e. a spoiled boy*

[14] With a good leg and a good foot   *Both of which are good for
dancing (actual and metaphorical).*

[16] 'a   *he*

[16–17] get her good will   *(1) get her acquiescence, or (2) be
desired by her. Will was often used to express motivation by the passions
rather than by the intellect (wit).*

[19] shrewd   *biting*

[20] curst   *sharp. As with* shrewd, *it implies both sarcastic wit and
acute understanding.*

[21–2] lessen God's sending   *reduce what God has given me*

[22–3] 'God . . . horns'   *A proverb suggesting the fair balance of
things: God sees to it that a cow with a vicious temper cannot inflict much
damage.*

[25–6] God will send you no horns   *Leonato is certainly aware of
another meaning for* horns, *as a phallic symbol. With too sharp a tongue, he
says, Beatrice won't be attractive to men.*

ACT TWO

Scene 1. *Enter* LEONATO, ANTONIO, HERO, BEATRICE, MARGARET *and* URSULA

LEONATO Was not Count John here at supper?

ANTONIO I saw him not.

BEATRICE How tartly that gentleman looks! I never can see him but I am heart-burned an hour after.

HERO He is of a very melancholy disposition.

BEATRICE He were an excellent man that were made just in the mid-way between him and Benedick – the one is too like an image and says nothing, and the other too like my lady's eldest son, evermore tattling.   10

LEONATO Then half Signor Benedick's tongue in Count John's mouth, and half Count John's melancholy in Signor Benedick's face –

BEATRICE With a good leg and a good foot, uncle, and money enough in his purse – such a man would win any woman in the world, if 'a could get her good will.

LEONATO By my troth, niece, thou wilt never get thee a husband if thou be so shrewd of thy tongue.

ANTONIO In faith, she's too curst.   20

BEATRICE Too curst is more than curst. I shall lessen God's sending that way, for it is said, 'God sends a curst cow short horns'; but to a cow too curst he sends none.

LEONATO So, by being too curst, God will send you no horns?

[27] Just   *exactly*

if he send me no husband   *Now she openly acknowledges* horns *as sexual.*

[31] in the woollen   *between rough blankets, or in a shroud*

[32] light on   *(1) come across (2) fall on. (Leonato is perfectly aware of the sexual pun he is making.)*

[33–4] that hath no beard   *i.e. who is not mature physically*

[34–6] Dress . . . gentlewoman   *Beatrice derides the idea of an 'unmasculine' husband.*

[36–9] He . . . him   *She wants someone who is youthful, and therefore physically energetic; but not young, in the sense of being physically immature (less than a man).*

[39–41] Therefore . . . hell   *i.e. if she can't get what she wants, she would rather stay unmarried. Leading apes into hell was the proverbial fate of women who died without losing their virginity (since those who had children could lead them into heaven). Clearly a fate devised by men.*

[40] in earnest   *as an advance payment*

bear-ward   *bear keeper. Apes were sometimes kept for baiting, along with bears.*

[44] like an old cuckold with horns   *Beatrice seems to see all horns as having sexual significance, even those of the devil. (For cuckold, see note on I.1.193–5.)*

[46] here's no place for you maids   *Her devil seems to be on the side of women!*

[48–9] He . . . long   *Her St Peter directs her to the unmarried men who are (naturally?) already in heaven. She could be seen as making a very modern objection to the stigma inherent in 'old maid' and the apparent respectability of 'bachelor'. In any case, she intends to enjoy herself.*

[48] bachelors   *Usually this meant unmarried men or women, but Shakespeare always uses it in reference to men.*

[51] ruled by   *advised by. Antonio might well feel anxious about the influence Beatrice could be having on Hero.*

[53–6] But . . . me   *That anxiety is immediately justified as Beatrice advises her cousin to be independent, if her father wants her to marry someone who is not attractive.*

[58] fitted   *mentally suited and physically matched (with a bawdy joke as well)*

[59–60] Not . . . earth   *This refers to the Creation (Genesis 2 : 7) in which God creates man from 'the dust of the ground'.*

BEATRICE Just, if he send me no husband; for the which blessing I am at him upon my knees every morning and evening. Lord, I could not endure a husband with a beard on his face – I had rather lie 30 in the woollen!

LEONATO You may light on a husband that hath no beard.

BEATRICE What should I do with him? Dress him in my apparel and make him my waiting gentlewoman? He that hath a beard is more than a youth; and he that hath no beard is less than a man – and he that is more than a youth is not for me, and he that is less than a man, I am not for him. Therefore I will even take sixpence in earnest of the bear-ward, 40 and lead his apes into hell.

LEONATO Well then, go you into hell?

BEATRICE No, but to the gate; and there will the devil meet me, like an old cuckold with horns on his head, and say, 'Get you to heaven, Beatrice, get you to heaven; here's no place for you maids'. So deliver I up my apes and away to Saint Peter for the heavens. He shows me where the bachelors sit, and there live we as merry as the day is long.

ANTONIO [*To* HERO] Well, niece, I trust you will be 50 ruled by your father.

BEATRICE Yes, faith, it is my cousin's duty to make curtsy and say, 'Father, as it please you'. But yet for all that, cousin, let him be a handsome fellow, or else make another curtsy and say, 'Father, as it please me'.

LEONATO [*To* BEATRICE] Well, niece, I hope to see you one day fitted with a husband.

BEATRICE Not till God make men of some other metal

[60–1] Would . . . dust *Since woman was made from man's rib and not from dust, Beatrice is suggesting inherent superiority.*

[61–2] to make . . . marl *to have to justify herself to a lump of clay*

[63] I'll none *i.e. I don't want a husband*

[63–5] Adam's . . . kindred *we're all related under Adam and I think it's a sin to marry a relative*

[67] solicit you in that kind *approach you about marriage*

[69–70] The fault . . . time *A complex metaphor: while appearing to refer to the dance, she is really talking about courtship; the music in that case becomes the thing which initiates it – the attraction or sex-drive.*

[70] in good time *(1) evenly (music) (2) with decorum (courtship)*

[70–1] too important *too rushed; important: importunate*

[71–2] tell . . . answer *tell him there is a time for everything and extend your answer the full length of the dance; measure: the set rhythm of the dance; dance out: dance fully*

[72] the answer *(1) your answer (see Leonato, l. 68, (2) your response (to him as a lover)*

[72–9] For . . . grave *Beatrice's famous definition of the three stages of love, each depicted as a dance, and a parody of Sir John Davies' poem,* Orchestra. [73] Scotch jig *A speedy, energetic dance.*

[74] measure *A stately dance with dignified, deliberate movements.* cinquepace *(apparently pronounced 'sink-a-pace') Another name for the galliard, a dance with five steps and a leap.* first suit *i.e. courtship*

[75] and full as fantastical *and just as fanciful*

[76] mannerly modest *utterly seemly* [77] ancientry *old formalities*

[78–9] falls . . . grave *She puns on* cinquepace, *with the image of the degenerating relationship as age increases, leading finally to the grave.*

[80] you . . . shrewdly *you have an acute understanding*

[81] eye *eyesight (as an observer and as someone on the look-out)*

[81–2] I can see a church by daylight *Her observations of life lead her to avoid a church (i.e. weddings) – during the daytime at any rate!*

[83–4] Make good room! *Asking everyone to spread out, ready to dance.*

[Enter DON PEDRO . . .] *Most of the men are masked; their entrance causes a great stir, though the women seem in no doubt as to identities. They might begin a slow dance, perhaps a set in which couples wait to take their turn, to allow for conversations. More probably, it is a time of mixing and settling partners, before the full dance (l. 152).*

than earth! Would it not grieve a woman to be 60
over-mastered with a piece of valiant dust? To
make an account of her life to a clod of wayward
marl? No, uncle, I'll none. Adam's sons are my
brethren, and truly I hold it a sin to match in my
kindred.

LEONATO Daughter, remember what I told you – if
the Prince do solicit you in that kind, you know
your answer.

BEATRICE The fault will be in the music, cousin, if you
be not wooed in good time. If the Prince be too 70
important, tell him there is measure in everything
and so dance out the answer. For hear me, Hero:
wooing, wedding and repenting is as a Scotch jig, a
measure and a cinquepace; the first suit is hot and
hasty like a Scotch jig, and full as fantastical; the
wedding mannerly modest, as a measure, full of
state and ancientry; and then comes repentance
and, with his bad legs, falls into the cinquepace
faster and faster, till he sink into his grave.

LEONATO Cousin, you apprehend passing shrewdly. 80

BEATRICE I have a good eye, uncle; I can see a church
by daylight.

LEONATO The revellers are entering, brother. Make
good room! [*He and* ANTONIO *put on masks*]

Enter DON PEDRO, CLAUDIO, BENEDICK, BALTHASAR,
DON JOHN, BORACHIO *and others (masked)*

The dance begins

DON PEDRO Lady, will you walk about with your
friend?

[86] friend   *lover; Don Pedro and Hero flirt openly, and Hero's responses are far from naïve.*

[87] So   *if*

[87–8] say nothing   *don't make improper suggestions; nothing = no thing, which has bawdy implications.*

[91] when I please   *if I want to (implying, when I find you attractive) or, when you fancy me.*

[93] favour   *(1) face (which she can't see at the moment), or (2) attractiveness*

[93–4] God . . . case   *Heaven forbid that you should look like your mask*

[95] visor   *mask*

[95–6] Philemon's . . . Jove   *He is referring to the story of the peasant who entertained Jove, the king of gods, in his simple cottage. (By likening himself to Jove, he implies that he has a strongly sexual nature.)*

[97] should be thatched   *i.e. like the cottage roof*

[98] Speak low if you speak love   *(1) lower your voice if you want to talk about love (2) if you are talking of love, you should talk of something lower than the thatch*

[99] BENEDICK   *There is no convincing reason for changing Margaret's partner to Balthasar as many editors have done. The conversation shows Benedick in the role of a 'lady's man' as his reputation has already indicated (see I.1.105) and the tone of their exchange is similar to that at V.2. The interruption by Balthasar leaves him free to find Beatrice.*

[101] ill   *bad*

[104] the hearers   *(Balthasar is obviously listening in)*

[106] God match me with a good dancer   *She is openly insulting Benedick about (1) his dancing, and (2) his potential as a lover.*

[107] Amen   *so be it; Balthasar is suggesting that he can fulfil those functions better.*

[108–9] And God . . .done   *when the fun's over, let him disappear (the implication being that she wants enjoyment, but not commitment)*

[109] Answer, clerk   *A stroke of arch-irreverence: she asks for an answer from the* clerk *(the man who led the responses in church) to her prayer, which runs directly against any idea of marriage.*

[110] No more words   *The emphasis would probably fall on* words, *implying that it was time to get on with the dancing.*

is answered   *has the answer he wants*

HERO So you walk softly and look sweetly and say
  nothing, I am yours for the walk; and especially
  when I walk away.

DON PEDRO With me in your company?   90

HERO I may say so, when I please.

DON PEDRO And when please you to say so?

HERO When I like your favour, for God defend the
  lute should be like the case!

DON PEDRO My visor is Philemon's roof; within the
  house is Jove.

HERO Why, then your visor should be thatched.

DON PEDRO Speak low if you speak love.

They move aside

BENEDICK Well, I would you did like me.

MARGARET So would not I, for your own sake, for 100
  I have many ill qualities.

BENEDICK Which is one?

MARGARET I say my prayers aloud.

BENEDICK I love you the better – the hearers may cry
  'Amen'.

MARGARET God match me with a good dancer!

BALTHASAR Amen.

MARGARET And God keep him out of my sight when
  the dance is done! Answer, clerk.

She changes partners

BALTHASAR No more words – the clerk is answered! 110

They move aside

URSULA I know you well enough – you are Signor
  Antonio.

[113] At a word   *briefly*

[115] counterfeit   *imitate*

[116] do him so ill-well   *represent his defects so convincingly*

[117] the very man   *the man himself*

his dry hand   *A sign of age – she is suggesting his dried-up physical capacities (damp hands were associated with a lecherous disposition).*

[117–18] up and down   *all over (she is probably stroking his hand)*

[120–3] Come . . . end   *She tries to flatter him into revealing his identity (*excellent wit, virtue, graces*) and is being ironical at his expense.*

[122] mum   *silence*

[122–3] graces will appear, and there's an end   *i.e. you can't hide good qualities, so I'm sure I'm right*

[125] you shall pardon me   *i.e. for refusing to tell you*

[129] the Hundred Merry Tales   *A book of humorous tales, mostly bawdy, published in 1526. The attack on her wit as being derived and not original hits hard, as do her retaliatory comments.*

[136–7] the Prince's jester, a very dull fool   *A jester or fool was a standard figure at court whose task was to keep the courtiers amused. Beatrice is saying that Benedick is playing that role, and playing it badly – a double insult.* dull: *stupid*

[137] only his gift   *the only thing he's capable of*

[138] None but libertines delight in him   *only the more debauched members of the court find him entertaining*

[139] the commendation . . . villainy   *they appreciate him for his coarseness rather than for his wit*

[140] he both pleases men and angers them   *he amuses them (with his insinuations) and annoys them (with his slanders)*

[141–2] in the fleet   *here in the assembled company*

[142] I would he had boarded me   *I wish he had accosted me (knowing full well that he has). Is she aware of the implication of her metaphor,* boarded?

ANTONIO At a word, I am not.

URSULA I know you by the waggling of your head.

ANTONIO To tell you true, I counterfeit him.

URSULA You could never do him so ill-well, unless you
were the very man. Here's his dry hand up and
down – you are he, you are he.

ANTONIO At a word, I am not.

URSULA Come, come, do you think I do not know you 120
by your excellent wit? Can virtue hide itself? Go to,
mum, you are he; graces will appear and there's an
end.

They move aside

BEATRICE Will you not tell me who told you so?

BENEDICK No, you shall pardon me.

BEATRICE Nor will you not tell me who you are?

BENEDICK Not now.

BEATRICE That I was disdainful, and that I had my
good wit out of the Hundred Merry Tales – well,
this was Signor Benedick that said so.   130

BENEDICK What's he?

BEATRICE I am sure you know him well enough.

BENEDICK Not I, believe me.

BEATRICE Did he never make you laugh?

BENEDICK I pray you, what is he?

BEATRICE Why, he is the Prince's jester, a very dull
fool – only his gift is in devising impossible slanders.
None but libertines delight in him, and the
commendation is not in his wit but in his villainy,
for he both pleases men and angers them; and then 140
they laugh at him and beat him. I am sure he is in
the fleet – I would he had boarded me.

[145–6] He'll . . . me   *i.e. he'll try unsuccessfully to be witty at my expense. Her image is of weapons which break, rather than strike effectively.*

[146–7] which . . . melancholy   *which will probably be neither noticed nor found amusing and so he'll be depressed*

[148] a partridge wing saved   *She is insulting him by suggesting that his normal appetite is small (since a partridge wing carries little meat). It is also insulting his potential as a lover, if appetite is taken metaphorically (see note at I.1.51).*

[149] the leaders   *of the dance (either the full dance begins here, or it is their turn to move if they have been waiting in line)*

[152] the next turning   *i.e. in the dance*

[Dance]   *Some editions of the play exclude the possibility of a full dance before the exit, which would deny the scene a major spectacle in terms of its production. The image created is powerful, in that the unity of this dance is disrupted by the division of the partners at the end (as indicated by Don John's comment at l. 155), which denotes that all is not yet settled.*

[Exeunt]   *The dance over, the destructive effects of the seeming truth now follow in its wake.*

[153–5] Sure . . . it   *Is Don John taken in or not? This could be said aloud, to cause trouble, or aside to Borachio, if he is really unsure. Whichever way, he can make trouble from it.*

[155] the ladies follow her   *Indicating the way the dancers leave the stage in separate columns.*

[157] his bearing   *the way he stands*

[160] You . . . he   *Claudio's motive for saying this is not clear, but it certainly fits in well with Don John's scheme.*

[161] very near   *very close to (as a confidant)*

[163] no equal for his birth   *not of the same social standing (would this seriously concern Don John?)*

[166] I heard him swear   *He builds the fabrication with apparent fact to make its 'truth' more convincing.*

[167–8] So . . . tonight   *Borachio confirms and develops the story.*

[169] banquet   *Not a full meal but a course of sweetmeats, fruit and wine, served as refreshment for the dancers.*

BENEDICK When I know the gentleman, I'll tell him what you say.

BEATRICE Do, do. He'll but break a comparison or two on me, which peradventure not marked or not laughed at, strikes him into melancholy; and then there's a partridge wing saved, for the fool will eat no supper that night. We must follow the leaders.

BENEDICK In every good thing.   150

BEATRICE Nay, if they lead to any ill, I will leave them at the next turning.

Dance

[*Exeunt all, dancing, but* DON JOHN, BORACHIO *and*
                                                    CLAUDIO

DON JOHN Sure my brother is amorous on Hero and hath withdrawn her father to break with him about it. The ladies follow her and but one visor remains.

BORACHIO [*Aside to* DON JOHN] And that is Claudio – I know him by his bearing.

DON JOHN [*To* CLAUDIO] Are not you Signor Benedick?

CLAUDIO You know me well, I am he.   160

DON JOHN Signor, you are very near my brother in his love. He is enamoured on Hero – I pray you dissuade him from her; she is no equal for his birth. You may do the part of an honest man in it.

CLAUDIO How know you he loves her?

DON JOHN I heard him swear his affection.

BORACHIO So did I too, and he swore he would marry her tonight.

DON JOHN Come, let us to the banquet.

                         [*Exeunt, leaving* CLAUDIO *alone*

CLAUDIO Thus answer I in name of Benedick   170

[172] 'Tis certain so   *Claudio's own suspicions find confirmation in Don John's words; he is an easy prey.*

[173-4] Friendship . . . love   *you can expect friends to be loyal in everything, except when it comes to anything to do with love. In his disappointment Claudio makes rapid judgements.*

[174] office   *business*

[175-6] Therefore . . . itself   *i.e. everyone in love should speak and plead for himself.* Heart *and* eye *are traditional sources of love; here they are personified to represent the lover.*

[177-8] for. . . blood   *The responsibility for changing trustworthiness into passion is seen as beauty's (a* witch). Witch *was also another word for whore.*

[179] an accident of hourly proof   *such a common occurrence*

[180] which I mistrusted not   *which I'd forgotten to be on the watch for*

Farewell therefore, Hero   *This rapid acceptance of the apparent change in his fortune prepares us for his behaviour later in the play.*

[185] Even to the next willow   *The willow, as the emblem of the forsaken lover, indicates immediately that Benedick has also been taken in by Don Pedro.*

[186] County   *Count*

What fashion   *how*

[187-8] an usurer's chain   *It was fashionable for rich men to wear gold chains; a* usurer *(or moneylender) became wealthy by charging high rates of interest. There is a pun in the idea that Claudio has 'lent' Hero to Don Pedro, and can now exact 'interest' of some kind.*

[188] a lieutenant's scarf   *the sash worn by soldiers, diagonally across the body from one shoulder (the implication being that Claudio should challenge Don Pedro to a duel)*

[189] one way   *i.e. one way or the other (payment must be exacted, since the fact is certain)*

[192] an honest drovier   *a good cattle dealer (who's just sold his calves). Benedick implies that Claudio should be angrier.*

[193] so   *that's how*

[194] served you thus   *treated you like this;* served *recalls Don Pedro's own words to Claudio at I.1.313, and in both cases there is an underlying bawdy pun on* serve, *a term used in animal husbandry for the mating of stock.*

But hear these ill news with the ears of Claudio.
'Tis certain so; the Prince woos for himself.
Friendship is constant in all other things,
Save in the office and affairs of love.
Therefore, all hearts in love use their own
    tongues;
Let every eye negotiate for itself,
And trust no agent – for beauty is a witch
Against whose charms faith melteth into blood.
This is an accident of hourly proof,
Which I mistrusted not. Farewell therefore,
    Hero!   180

Enter BENEDICK

BENEDICK Count Claudio?
CLAUDIO Yea, the same.
BENEDICK Come, will you go with me?
CLAUDIO Whither?
BENEDICK Even to the next willow, about your own
  business, County. What fashion will you wear the
  garland of? About your neck, like an usurer's
  chain? Or under your arm like a lieutenant's scarf?
  You must wear it one way, for the Prince hath got
  your Hero.   190
CLAUDIO I wish him joy of her.
BENEDICK Why, that's spoken like an honest drovier;
  so they sell bullocks. But did you think the Prince
  would have served you thus?
CLAUDIO I pray you, leave me.

He thrusts him roughly aside

73

[196–8] Now . . . post   *i.e. you've got the wrong man (strike suggests that Claudio is really angry)*

[201] sedges   *reed-like grasses (for safe cover)*

[201–7] But that . . . may   *Benedick is really much more concerned about the insults Beatrice has hurled at him.*

[202–3] It may . . . merry   *He is worried enough about his public image to examine her accusations seriously.*

[203] go . . . title   *have that reputation*   merry   *light-hearted*

[204] but . . . wrong   *but by supposing this, I am too ready to find fault with myself*

[204–5] I . . . reputed   *that's not my reputation (He is on the point of believing her before he decides it is merely her way of distorting things.)*

[205] the base though bitter disposition   *A phrase that has caused much editorial discussion. The sense seems to be, 'It's unusually low for her, even though she is usually sarcastic'.*

[206] that . . . person   *makes it seem as if she is only repeating what is thought by many*   [207] gives me out   *talks about me*

[Enter DON PEDRO]   *The original stage directions here are confused and brought on many characters, including Hero and Leonato. Many editors still retain their entrance, but there are strong arguments for delaying it: they don't speak for a long time; they would be unlikely, if listening, to keep silent; there is nothing in the conversation that they need to know. Hence, it seems better to bring them on at a time when Claudio knows his match is secured. Leonato can then burst in cheerfully with his formal approval.*

[210] Troth   *in truth*   [211] Lady Fame   *a personification of rumour (such an essential element in the play)*

[211–12] as . . . warren   *as sad as a house in the middle of a park, i.e. miserably solitary. Perhaps a literary joke about a poem by Sir Thomas Lodge.*

[212–13] I think I told him true   *This appears to confirm Benedick's ignorance of the plan (see back to l. 185).*

[213] this   *Even without Hero's presence this is acceptable; she could be indicated with a gesture.*

[216] or to bind him up a rod   *(not a true report of what he said)*

[219] flat transgression   *stupid mistake. To Benedick's cynical view, the person who trusts another is the fool.*

[221] steals   *Pronounced 'stales' at this time, and hence a pun; stale: prostitute*

[223] The . . . stealer   *Presumably Don Pedro is well aware that he is identifying himself as the 'transgressor'.*

BENEDICK Ho! Now you strike like the blind man;
  'twas the boy that stole your meat and you'll beat
  the post.

CLAUDIO If it will not be, I'll leave you.

[*Exit*

BENEDICK Alas, poor hurt fowl, now will he creep into 200
  sedges. But that my Lady Beatrice should know me
  and not know me – the Prince's fool? Hah! It may
  be I go under that title because I am merry. Yea,
  but so I am apt to do myself wrong. I am not so
  reputed. It is the base though bitter disposition of
  Beatrice that puts the world into her person, and so
  gives me out. Well, I'll be revenged as I may.

Enter DON PEDRO

DON PEDRO Now, signor, where's the Count? Did you
  see him?

BENEDICK Troth, my lord, I have played the part of 210
  Lady Fame. I found him here as melancholy as a
  lodge in a warren. I told him, and I think I told him
  true, that your grace had got the good will of this
  young lady; and I offered him my company to a
  willow tree, either to make him a garland, as being
  forsaken, or to bind him up a rod, as being worthy
  to be whipped.

DON PEDRO To be whipped? What's his fault?

BENEDICK The flat transgression of a schoolboy who,
  being overjoyed with finding a bird's nest, shows it 220
  his companion, and he steals it.

DON PEDRO Wilt thou make a trust a transgression?
  The transgression is in the stealer.

BENEDICK Yet it had not been amiss the rod had been

[227] bestowed on you   *struck you with (literally, given to you)*
take   *(1) hear (2) a pun on* take *in the sense of steal*
[229] them   *i.e. the fledglings in the nest*
sing   *Teaching the birds to sing is a metaphor here for teaching Hero to be responsive to her lover.*
[231] if . . . saying   *if she proves'that (by responding to Claudio)*
[232] honestly   *(1) truthfully (2) not guilty of seducing her*
[233] The Lady Beatrice   *Don Pedro changes the subject – in hope of more entertainment?*
(236–57) O, she misused . . . her   *This whole speech is notable for its emphatic exasperation.*
[237] block   *(of wood)* but ... leaf   *i.e. only just alive*
[238] answered her   *engaged in argument with her*
my very visor   *my mask itself*
[239] not thinking   *He is mistaken about this of course.*
[241] duller than a great thaw   *i.e. something which has none of the brilliance of fresh snow – Benedick continues to elaborate her insults.*
[241–2] huddling . . . jest   *heaping up one jest after another (on me)*
[242] impossible conveyance   *incredible dexterity*
[243] at a mark   *at the target. His simile shows her effectiveness.*
[244] poniards   *daggers*
[245–6] If . . . terminations   *if her breath was as awful as her words*
[247] to   *as far as*
[247–8] I would not marry her   *Has the possibility occurred to him? This is also for emphasis; he won't marry her even if her dowry is the Garden of Eden!*
[249–50] She . . . spit   *she'd have forced the great Hercules to do menial jobs (like turning the spit to roast the meat). Hercules was the Greek hero of legendary strength who usually performed spectacular tasks.*
[250] yea, and . . . too   *she would even have split up his (famous) club for firewood*
[252] Ate   *goddess of Discord (usually depicted in rags)*
in good apparel   *well-dressed. Perhaps an acknowledgement of how Beatrice looks (compare I.1.187) but primarily implying that there is a discrepancy between how she appears, and what she actually is.*
[253] conjure her   *exorcise her. Only a scholar would know the Latin necessary for the incantations!*
[253–5] for . . . sanctuary   *compared to being in her presence even hell is like a quiet retreat*   [256] would   *want to*

made, and the garland too. For the garland he
might have worn himself, and the rod he might
have bestowed on you, who (as I take it) have stolen
his bird's nest.

DON PEDRO I will but teach them to sing and restore
them to the owner.   230

BENEDICK If their singing answer your saying, by my
faith you say honestly.

DON PEDRO The Lady Beatrice hath a quarrel to you –
the gentleman that danced with her told her she is
much wronged by you.

BENEDICK O, she misused me past the endurance of a
block! An oak but with one green leaf on it would
have answered her – my very visor began to assume
life and scold with her. She told me, not thinking I
had been myself, that I was the Prince's jester, that 240
I was duller than a great thaw; huddling jest upon
jest with such impossible conveyance upon me, that
I stood like a man at a mark, with a whole army
shooting at me. She speaks poniards and every word
stabs. If her breath were as terrible as her
terminations, there were no living near her; she
would infect to the north star. I would not marry
her though she were endowed with all that Adam
had left him before he transgressed. She would have
made Hercules have turned spit, yea and have cleft 250
his club to make the fire too. Come, talk not of her –
you shall find her the infernal Ate, in good apparel.
I would to God some scholar would conjure her; for
certainly, while she is here, a man may live as quiet
in hell as in a sanctuary, and people sin upon
purpose because they would go thither; so indeed
all disquiet, horror, and perturbation follows her.

[259] Will your grace . . . me   *After the emphatic denunciations, this speech reaches a climax in desperation as Beatrice appears, and Benedick rapidly asks to be sent on ludicrous missions.*

[260] slightest   *most trivial*

[262] tooth-picker   *An ordinary tooth-pick.*

[264] Prester John   *The legendary priest-king, supposed to have ruled in a remote area of Asia or Africa.*

[264–5] the great Cham   *Ruler of the Mongols.*

[265] embassage   *errand*

[266] Pigmies   *A legendary race of dwarfs thought to live in Africa or Asia. The Pigmy race itself was unknown then, although dwarf races occur several times in early literature.*

[267] harpy   *In Greek mythology a harpy was a hideous monster (a woman's head with a bird's body), which caused destruction and havoc.*

[270] Lady Tongue   *Beatrice, referred to by her dominant characteristic; with a pun in connection with* dish – a dish I love not *can also mean a woman he doesn't fancy.*

[274] use for it   *paid him interest (usury)*

a double . . . one   *i.e. the 'loan' cost twice as much as it was worth; also implying her duplicity.*

[275] once before . . . dice   *Another reference to their previous relationship; seemingly Beatrice came off worse that time.*

[277] put him down   *got the better of him*

[280] lest . . . fools   *in case it would result in having stupid children (she takes* put down *literally)*

[280–1] I . . . seek   *A reference to an off-stage direction, which makes sense of her entrance with Claudio.*

Enter CLAUDIO *and* BEATRICE

DON PEDRO Look, here she comes.

BENEDICK Will your grace command me any service
to the world's end? I will go on the slightest errand, 260
now, to the Antipodes, that you can devise to send
me on. I will fetch you a tooth-picker, now, from
the furthest inch of Asia – bring you the length of
Prester John's foot – fetch you a hair off the great
Cham's beard – do you any embassage to the
Pigmies – rather than hold three words' conference
with this harpy. You have no employment for me?

DON PEDRO None, but to desire your good company.

BENEDICK O God, sir, here's a dish I love not; I
cannot endure my Lady Tongue.   270
                                                              [*Exit*

DON PEDRO Come lady, come, you have lost the heart of
Signor Benedick.

BEATRICE Indeed, my lord, he lent it me a while and I
gave him use for it, a double heart for his single one.
Marry, once before he won it of me, with false dice;
therefore your grace may well say I have lost it.

DON PEDRO You have put him down, lady, you have
put him down.

BEATRICE So I would not he should do me, my lord,
lest I should prove the mother of fools. I have 280
brought Count Claudio, whom you sent me to seek.

DON PEDRO Why, how now, Count – wherefore are
you sad?

CLAUDIO Not sad, my lord.

DON PEDRO How then? Sick?

CLAUDIO Neither, my lord.

BEATRICE The Count is neither sad, nor sick, nor

[288] civil Count, civil as an orange   *One of Beatrice's most famous puns, turning* civil *(serious) to Seville, which was spelt 'Civill' at the time.*

[289] jealous complexion   *Yellow was thought to denote jealousy. We have to assume that Beatrice has heard about his jealousy through gossip, or perhaps from Claudio himself.*

[290] blazon   *description; from heraldry, a device on a shield*

[291] if he be so   *i.e. jealous*

conceit   *idea*

[293–6] Here . . . joy   *As Leonato and Hero enter, Don Pedro quickly explains what has happened. (For a note on their entrance here, see back to l. 207)*

[299] all Grace   *i.e. God*

[301–2] Silence . . . much   *Claudio might well be stuck for words at this sudden change in his fortunes.*

[308] poor fool   *A term of affection.*

[309] windy side   *i.e. to windward. A nautical metaphor: sailing ships had the advantage if they kept up-wind of the enemy.*

[312] Good Lord for alliance   *i.e. hooray for marriage (she is exclaiming at Claudio calling her* cousin)

[312–13] Thus goes . . . world   *i.e. everyone gets married*

[313] I am sunburnt   *I'm left out; literally, left out of doors and brown-skinned, and therefore unattractive (since for Elizabethans a pale skin was a mark of beauty); and because she is unattractive, she is left out of the marriage round. The result of the literal meaning becomes the cause of the metaphorical meaning – a good example of her sophisticated word-play.*

[314] Heigh ho for a husband   *Apparently the title of an old ballad.*

[315] get   *find*

[316–17] one of your father's getting   *i.e. someone like you; she takes* get *to mean beget; and uses* got *in the same way.*

merry, nor well, but civil Count, civil as an orange; and something of that jealous complexion.

DON PEDRO I'faith, lady, I think your blazon to be 290 true, though I'll be sworn, if he be so, his conceit is false.

Enter LEONATO *and* HERO

Here, Claudio, I have wooed in thy name and fair Hero is won; I have broke with her father and his good will obtained. Name the day of marriage, and God give thee joy!

LEONATO Count, take of me my daughter and with her my fortunes. His grace hath made the match and all Grace say Amen to it!

BEATRICE Speak, Count, 'tis your cue. 300

CLAUDIO Silence is the perfectest herald of joy; I were but little happy if I could say how much. Lady, as you are mine, I am yours. I give away myself for you and dote upon the exchange.

BEATRICE Speak, cousin; or, if you cannot, stop his mouth with a kiss and let not him speak neither.

DON PEDRO In faith, lady, you have a merry heart.

BEATRICE Yea, my lord, I thank it, poor fool; it keeps on the windy side of care. My cousin tells him in his ear that he is in her heart. 310

CLAUDIO And so she doth, cousin.

BEATRICE Good Lord for alliance! Thus goes every one to the world but I, and I am sunburnt; I may sit in a corner and cry 'Heigh ho for a husband'!

DON PEDRO Lady Beatrice, I will get you one.

BEATRICE I would rather have one of your father's getting – hath your grace ne'er a brother like you?

[322] too costly to wear   *She speaks as though he were an expensive set of clothes – thus neatly acknowledging that he is of higher social rank.*
[324] no matter   *no substance*
[325] Your . . . me   *I'd be more offended if you stayed silent*
[328] my mother cried   *i.e. in childbirth*
[329] a star danced   *Thought by astrologers to dictate a happy temperament (compare I.3.11); also particularly apt for Beatrice.*

[331–2] will . . . of   *A tactical reminder of some instructions given before this scene; Leonato is perhaps anxious about what Beatrice might say next. Now that the marriage is arranged he would naturally want to stop anything that might upset it.*
[333] cry you mercy   *beg your pardon*
[336–40] There's . . . laughing   *He is at pains to explain her character with this picture of constant gaiety.*
[336] melancholy element   *Each bodily humour (see note at I.1.129) was thought to correspond to an element (earth, fire, air or water).*
[338] not ever   *not always*

[341–2] hear tell of a husband   *the idea of marriage*
[344] out of suit   *into withdrawing their petitions (to her)*
[345] were   *would be*

Your father got excellent husbands, if a maid could come by them.

DON PEDRO Will you have me, lady?   320

BEATRICE No, my lord, unless I might have another for working days; your grace is too costly to wear every day. But I beseech your grace pardon me; I was born to speak all mirth and no matter.

DON PEDRO Your silence most offends me, and to be merry best becomes you; for, out a' question, you were born in a merry hour.

BEATRICE No, sure, my lord, my mother cried; but then there was a star danced and under that was I born. Cousins, God give you joy!   330

LEONATO Niece, will you look to those things I told you of?

BEATRICE I cry you mercy, uncle. By your grace's pardon.

[*Exit*

DON PEDRO By my troth, a pleasant-spirited lady.

LEONATO There's little of the melancholy element in her, my lord. She is never sad but when she sleeps, and not ever sad then, for I have heard my daughter say she hath often dreamed of unhappiness and waked herself with laughing.   340

DON PEDRO She cannot endure to hear tell of a husband?

LEONATO O, by no means – she mocks all her wooers out of suit.

DON PEDRO She were an excellent wife for Benedick.

LEONATO O Lord, my lord! If they were but a week married they would talk themselves mad.

DON PEDRO County Claudio, when mean you to go to church?

[350–1] Time ... rites   *The traditional impatience of the lover; with a play on* rites, *ceremonial and physical.*

[354] answer my mind   *as I want them*

[356] breathing   *delay*

[358] Hercules' labours   *i.e. tasks of extreme difficulty. In the legend, Hercules had twelve such tasks to perform to gain his freedom.*

[360–1] I would ... fashion it   *Again Don Pedro intends to play a major role in organising a match, and he is confident of success.*

[365] watchings   *sleeplessness*

[368] any modest office   *(1) anything within reason (2) anything moral. She is perfectly conscious of the pun on* modest, *in consenting to play a part which will amount to being a go-between for lovers.*

[372] approved   *tested*

[376] practise on   *Compare I.1.323, and II.2.52, and see Introduction, p. 8.*

[377] queasy stomach   *reluctance to become involved emotionally*

[379–80] we are the only love-gods   *A cheerful piece of boasting.*

[381] drift   *plan*

CLAUDIO Tomorrow, my lord. Time goes on crutches 350
till Love have all his rites.

LEONATO Not till Monday, my dear son, which is
hence a just seven-night and a time too brief too, to
have all things answer my mind.

DON PEDRO Come, you shake the head at so long a
breathing, but I warrant thee, Claudio, the time
shall not go dully by us. I will in the interim
undertake one of Hercules' labours, which is to
bring Signor Benedick and the Lady Beatrice into a
mountain of affection, th'one with th'other. I would 360
fain have it a match and I doubt not but to fashion
it, if you three will but minister such assistance as I
shall give you direction.

LEONATO My lord, I am for you, though it cost me ten
nights' watchings.

CLAUDIO And I, my lord.

DON PEDRO And you too, gentle Hero?

HERO I will do any modest office, my lord, to help my
cousin to a good husband.

DON PEDRO And Benedick is not the unhopefullest 370
husband that I know. Thus far can I praise him: he
is of a noble strain, of approved valour and
confirmed honesty. I will teach you how to humour
your cousin, that she shall fall in love with
Benedick; and I, with your two helps, will so
practise on Benedick that, in despite of his quick wit
and his queasy stomach, he shall fall in love with
Beatrice. If we can do this, Cupid is no longer an
archer; his glory shall be ours, for we are the only
love-gods! Go in with me, and I will tell you my 380
drift.

[*Exeunt*

ACT TWO, scene 2

To off-set the apparent settlement in II. 1, Don John now arranges with Borachio the specific detail of his design. They meet outside Leonato's house.

[1] shall   *is going to*

[3] cross   *thwart*

[5] medicinable to me   *act like a cure for me; characteristically Don John's cures are all negative*

sick in displeasure   *i.e. the reason he needs such 'medicines'*

[6–7] whatsoever . . . mine   *anything that disadvantages him (by spoiling his love) suits me very well*

[9] honestly   *openly*

covertly   *deceitfully*

[12] since   *ago*

[16] unseasonable instant   *strange hour*

[17] appoint   *arrange for*

[19–20] What . . . marriage   *how will that fact spoil this marriage. Life is deliberately used to contrast and highlight his aim.*

[21] The . . . temper   *the poison in this it is your responsibility to mix*

[22] spare not to tell him   *tell him in no uncertain terms*

[23] in marrying   *in arranging the marriage of*

[24–5] whose . . . up   *for whom you must extravagantly declare your high esteem*

[25] contaminated   *(1) morally impure (2) as a prostitute (stale) potentially diseased*

[28] misuse   *deceive*

vex   *torment*

[29] undo   *ruin*

[29–30] look . . . issue   *After such a catalogue of damage, the tone of this is very dry; black humour again.*

[31–2] Only . . . anything   *I'll try anything just to harm them; Don John's commitments are to malice, the reverse side of loyalty.*

Scene 2. *Enter* DON JOHN *and* BORACHIO

DON JOHN It is so. The Count Claudio shall marry the
daughter of Leonato.

BORACHIO Yea, my lord; but I can cross it.

DON JOHN Any bar, any cross, any impediment will be
medicinable to me. I am sick in displeasure to him,
and whatsoever comes athwart his affection ranges
evenly with mine. How canst thou cross this
marriage?

BORACHIO Not honestly, my lord, but so covertly that
no dishonesty shall appear in me.   10

DON JOHN Show me briefly how.

BORACHIO I think I told your lordship a year since
how much I am in the favour of Margaret, the
waiting gentlewoman to Hero?

DON JOHN I remember.

BORACHIO I can, at any unseasonable instant of the
night, appoint her to look out at her lady's chamber
window.

DON JOHN What life is in that, to be the death of this
marriage?   20

BORACHIO The poison of that lies in you to temper. Go
you to the Prince your brother; spare not to tell him
that he hath wronged his honour in marrying the
renowned Claudio – whose estimation do you
mightily hold up – to a contaminated stale, such a
one as Hero.

DON JOHN What proof shall I make of that?

BORACHIO Proof enough to misuse the Prince, to vex
Claudio, to undo Hero and kill Leonato – look you
for any other issue?   30

DON JOHN Only to despite them I will endeavour
anything.

[33] meet   *suitable*

[35–6] intend a kind of zeal   *pretend to be very concerned*

[36] as in love of   *caring for*

[38] thus like   *for this reason, likely*

[39] cozened . . . maid   *fooled by the fact that she appears virtuous*

[40] discovered thus   *revealed this to them*

[41] trial   *proof*

instances   *actual examples*

[42] bear . . . see   *be as real as seeing*

[43–4] hear me . . . Claudio   *For two reasons: (1) Margaret could easily be persuaded to take part innocently in the parody; (2) to the watchers, 'Hero' would appear more despicable.*

[46–7] I . . . absent   *It is not clear how he manages this detail.*

[48] disloyalty   *unfaithfulness*

[49] jealousy . . . assurance   *the jealous mind will turn the convincing appearance to a certainty*

[51–2] Grow . . . practice   *however bad the outcome I'll go ahead with the scheme (Note how this practice is a perverse parallel to Don Pedro's uses of the 'seeming truth': compare I.i.323, II.i.376.)*

[54] constant   *consistent*

[56] presently   *immediately*

ACT TWO, scene 3

Still reeling from the evil of Don John's agreed plan, we are immediately involved in the first part of Don Pedro's practice in which Benedick is the 'victim'. The spectacle of him being played like a hooked fish is predominantly funny, but not without serious undertones added by the perspective of Don John's proposed misuse of a similar manipulation. The scene takes place in the orchard of Leonato's house, which has already featured as a place where things are overheard (see I. 2).

BORACHIO Go, then; find me a meet hour to draw
Don Pedro and the Count Claudio alone. Tell them
that you know that Hero loves me; intend a kind of
zeal both to the Prince and Claudio – as in love of
your brother's honour who hath made this match,
and his friend's reputation, who is thus like to be
cozened with the semblance of a maid – that you
have discovered thus. They will scarcely believe this   40
without trial. Offer them instances, which shall
bear no less likelihood than to see me at her
chamber window, hear me call Margaret Hero,
hear Margaret term me Claudio. And bring them
to see this the very night before the intended
wedding – for in the meantime, I will so fashion the
matter that Hero shall be absent, and there shall
appear such seeming truth of Hero's disloyalty that
jealousy shall be called assurance, and all the
preparation overthrown.   50

DON JOHN Grow this to what adverse issue it can, I will
put it in practice. Be cunning in the working this,
and thy fee is a thousand ducats.

BORACHIO Be you constant in the accusation, and my
cunning shall not shame me.

DON JOHN I will presently go learn their day of
marriage.

[Exeunt

Scene 3. *Enter* BENEDICK

BENEDICK Boy!

Enter BOY

BOY Signor?

[3] in my chamber window   *i.e. on the window seat*

[5] I am here already   *Compare the phrase 'no sooner said than done'.*

[11-12] become . . . scorn   *become the focus of his own former condemnations*

[12] such a man is   *that's just what's happened to*

[13-14] there . . . fife   *he wasn't interested in any sound except music to march to; fife: a small flute*

[15] the tabor and the pipe   *music to dance to; tabor: a small drum*

[17] armour   *(suit of)*

[18] carving . . . doublet   *designing new clothes. A doublet was the tight garment worn by men to cover the top half of the body; it was often very ornate.*

[20] orthography   *precise spelling; here it stands for an elaborate, painstaking style.*

[21] fantastical   *very fanciful*

[23] I think not   *His assumption is of course full of dramatic irony; compare with the end of the scene.*

[25] I'll . . . oath   *i.e. he's sure, though, that until he is 'made an oyster' he won't be made a fool of by love (an elaborate way of saying 'it will never happen'). Oysters have long been considered aphrodisiac and there are other more bawdy connotations as well.*

[27] yet I am well   *despite that I'm still intact*

[30] grace   *favour (pun on graces)*

[30-5] Rich she . . . God   *Benedick now asserts his requirements.*

[31] never cheapen her   *literally, not bargain for her; also the sense of reducing her 'worth', by taking her virginity.*

[33] noble . . . angel   *He is punning on the names of Elizabethan coins; she must be noble or he won't touch her even if he's paid. (A noble was worth less than an angel.)*

[34-5] and her hair . . . God   *i.e. may her hair colour be natural (not dyed)*

BENEDICK In my chamber window lies a book – bring it hither to me in the orchard.

BOY I am here already, sir.

BENEDICK I know that, but I would have thee hence and here again.

[*Exit* BOY

I do much wonder that one man, seeing how much another man is a fool when he dedicates his behaviours to love, will, after he hath laughed at   10
such shallow follies in others, become the argument of his own scorn by falling in love; and such a man is Claudio. I have known when there was no music with him but the drum and the fife, and now had he rather hear the tabor and the pipe. I have known when he would have walked ten mile afoot to see a good armour; and now will he lie ten nights awake carving the fashion of a new doublet. He was wont to speak plain and to the purpose (like an honest man and a soldier) and now is he turned orthog-   20
raphy; his words are a very fantastical banquet, just so many strange dishes. May I be so converted and see with these eyes? I cannot tell; I think not. I will not be sworn but love may transform me to an oyster; but I'll take my oath on it, till he have made an oyster of me, he shall never make me such a fool. One woman is fair, yet I am well; another is wise, yet I am well; another virtuous, yet I am well. But till all graces be in one woman, one woman shall not come in my grace. Rich she shall be, that's certain;   30
wise, or I'll none; virtuous, or I'll never cheapen her; fair, or I'll never look on her; mild, or come not near me; noble, or not I for an angel; of good discourse, an excellent musician – and her hair shall

[36] Monsieur Love   *A mocking name for Claudio.*

[39] As . . . harmony   *as if it were deliberately quiet to complement the music (a romantic notion)*

[40] DON PEDRO [Aside]   *From here, Don Pedro, Claudio and Leonato comment aside to each other about the progress they are making, while Benedick's asides are for the audience only.*

[42] We'll . . . pennyworth   *we'll give the cunning so-and-so his money's worth (also bawdy; cf. the phrase 'tickle his fancy')*

[44] tax not . . . voice   *don't press me. His coyness has a teasing quality, as well as the conventional modesty of the performer.*

[45] slander   *disgrace*

[46] witness   *proof*

[47] To put a strange face on   *not to recognise*

[50–2] Since . . . loves   *The implication is that many swear love when they are really only after what they can get.* Yet: *still*

[53] hold longer argument   *prolong the discussion*

[54–5] Note . . . noting   *(He starts the play on* note *and* noting*) before I play* take heed of this: *there isn't a note of mine that is worth listening to*

be of what colour it please God. Ha, the Prince and
Monsieur Love! I will hide me in the arbour.

[*He hides*

Enter DON PEDRO, LEONATO and CLAUDIO

DON PEDRO Come, shall we hear this music?
CLAUDIO Yea, my good lord. How still the evening
    is,
  As hushed on purpose to grace harmony!
DON PEDRO [*Aside*] See you where Benedick hath
    hid himself?   40
CLAUDIO [*Aside*] O, very well, my lord. The music
    ended,
  We'll fit the hid-fox with a pennyworth.

Enter BALTHASAR, *with music*

DON PEDRO [*Aloud*] Come, Balthasar, we'll hear that
    song again.
BALTHASAR O good my lord, tax not so bad a voice
  To slander music any more than once.
DON PEDRO It is the witness still of excellency
  To put a strange face on his own perfection.
  I pray thee sing, and let me woo no more.
BALTHASAR Because you talk of wooing, I will sing,
  Since many a wooer doth commence his suit   50
  To her he thinks not worthy; yet he woos,
  Yet will he swear he loves.
DON PEDRO   Nay, pray thee come.
  Or if thou wilt hold longer argument,
  Do it in notes.
BALTHASAR   Note this before my notes,
  There's not a note of mine that's worth the
    noting.

[56] crotchets *(1) mere nothings (2) the short musical note itself*

[57] Note . . . nothing *Either a command – Don Pedro wants him to get to the point and play (and nothing else); or an exclamation at Balthasar's punning, quoting him.* Nothing *was pronounced the same as* noting.

[58–9] Now. . . ravished *He is being sarcastic at Claudio's expense.*

[59] sheep's guts *Used to make the strings on the lute. Benedick is deliberately undermining the beauty by this literal reference.*

[60] hale *drag*

[60–1] a horn . . . done *(1) I'd rather hear a hunting horn (2) it all leads to horns (see note on I.1.193).*

[BALTHASAR *sings*] *The song itself provides an interlude as well as presenting a judgement on men, which is going to prove apt in several different ways.*

[64] One . . . shore *they have the best of both worlds (with an underlying bawdy implication)*

[65] constant never *(as will soon be proved)*

[67] blithe and bonny *carefree and happy*

[70] moe *more*

[71] dumps *mournful songs*

[73] Since . . . leavy *i.e. since the beginning of time*

[77] hey nonny, nonny *The refrain invites carefree unconcern; it was often used suggestively.*

[79] ill *bad*

[81] shift *makeshift, either in place of anyone better, or as being without rehearsal*

[82] An *if*

DON PEDRO Why, these are very crotchets that he
    speaks;
    Note notes, forsooth, and nothing.

Music

BENEDICK [*Aside*] Now, divine air! Now is his soul
ravished! Is it not strange that sheep's guts should
hale souls out of men's bodies? Well, a horn for my 60
money, when all's done.

BALTHASAR *sings*

    Sigh no more, ladies, sigh no more,
      Men were deceivers ever;
    One foot in sea, and one on shore,
      To one thing constant never.
    Then sigh not so, but let them go
      And be you blithe and bonny,
    Converting all your sounds of woe
      Into hey nonny, nonny,

    Sing no more ditties, sing no moe   70
      Of dumps so dull and heavy,
    The fraud of men was ever so
      Since Summer first was leavy.
    Then sigh not so, but let them go
      And be you blithe and bonny,
    Converting all your sounds of woe
      Into hey nonny, nonny.

DON PEDRO By my troth, a good song.
BALTHASAR And an ill singer, my lord.
DON PEDRO Ha, no, no; faith, thou sing'st well enough 80
    for a shift.
BENEDICK [*Aside*] An he had been a dog that should

[84] bode no mischief *isn't a bad omen*
[85] as lief *as soon*
night-raven *A bird of uncertain species whose night-cry was thought to predict disaster. Benedick's disdain of the singing might really be a reaction to the song's suggestion that it is men who are inconstant, rather than women.*
[88–9] for tomorrow night *A reminder that the week is passing.*

[93] Come hither, Leonato *Don Pedro now begins his 'Herculean labour' (see II.1.358).*
[96] stalk on *A metaphor drawn from wild-fowling, in which a stalking-horse (real or artificial) was used to hide the fowler as he approached the bird.*

[99] wonderful *amazing*

[101] in all outward behaviours *i.e. to all appearances*
[102] abhor *loathe*
[103–4] Sits . . . corner *is that how things really are (literally: is that where the wind's coming from)*
[106–7] enraged affection *very passionately*
[107] it . . . thought *it's past anything the mind can reach*
[108] counterfeit *pretend*

[111–12] so near the life of passion *i.e. so like the real thing*
[112] discovers *reveals*
[114] Bait . . . bite *Another sporting metaphor.*

have howled thus, they would have hanged him; and I pray God his bad voice bode no mischief. I had as lief have heard the night-raven, come what plague could have come after it.

DON PEDRO Yea, marry, dost thou hear, Balthasar? I pray thee, get us some excellent music, for tomorrow night we would have it at the Lady Hero's chamber window.   90

BALTHASAR The best I can, my lord.

DON PEDRO Do so; farewell.

[*Exit* BALTHASAR

Come hither, Leonato. What was it you told me of today, that your niece, Beatrice, was in love with Signor Benedick?

CLAUDIO [*Aside*] O ay, stalk on, stalk on, the fowl sits. [*Aloud*] I did never think that lady would have loved any man.

LEONATO No, nor I neither, but most wonderful that she should so dote on Signor Benedick, whom she 100 hath, in all outward behaviours, seemed ever to abhor.

BENEDICK [*Aside*] Is't possible? Sits the wind in that corner?

LEONATO By my troth, my lord, I cannot tell what to think of it, but that she loves him with an enraged affection – it is past the infinite of thought.

DON PEDRO Maybe she doth but counterfeit?

CLAUDIO Faith, like enough.

LEONATO O God, counterfeit? There was never 110 counterfeit of passion came so near the life of passion as she discovers it.

DON PEDRO Why, what effects of passion shows she?

CLAUDIO [*Aside*] Bait the hook well, this fish will bite.

[115] **What effects, my lord** *He is playing for time. On stage, the ensuing exchange is great fun as each of them tries to keep the invention going; Leonato is not as quick as the other two.*

[119-20] **invincible . . . affection** *This is in Don Pedro's usual metaphor, giving the image of Beatrice besieged by declarations, but insuperable.*

[122] **especially against Benedick** *i.e. particularly resistant to his advances*

[123] **gull** *attempt to trick me*
but that *except for the fact that*

[124-5] **Knavery . . . reverence** *surely a man of his age (dignity) would not take part in such a trick (Benedick is deceived by Leonato's appearance.)*

[126] **the infection** *the* bait *now becomes a disease – compare I.1.87; I.1.314; III.4.71 and elsewhere*
hold *keep*

[131] **her torment** *what gives her such pain*

[132-4] **'Tis . . . him** *Claudio's inventiveness expands into dramatisation with this piece of reported dialogue; Leonato takes his cue from* write.

[137] **smock** *an undergarment also worn as a nightdress*
writ *written*

[138] **My . . . all** *Another play for time.*

[140] **jest** *joke*

[142-3] **between the sheet** *Leonato comes back with the pun on* sheet *as paper and bed-sheet.*

[146] **halfpence** *i.e. tiny pieces*
railed at *scolded*

[147] **immodest** *lacking in pride (with a pun in conjunction with* sheet, *lacking in modesty)*
flout *scorn*

LEONATO What effects, my lord? She will sit you – you heard my daughter tell you how.

CLAUDIO She did indeed.

DON PEDRO How, how, I pray you? You amaze me; I would have thought her spirit had been invincible against all assaults of affection.   120

LEONATO I would have sworn it had, my lord, especially against Benedick.

BENEDICK [*Aside*] I should think this a gull but that the white-bearded fellow speaks it. Knavery cannot, sure, hide himself in such reverence.

CLAUDIO [*Aside*] He hath ta'en the infection; hold it up.

DON PEDRO Hath she made her affection known to Benedick?

LEONATO No, and swears she never will – that's her 130 torment.

CLAUDIO 'Tis true indeed, so your daughter says. 'Shall I,' says she, 'that have so oft encountered him with scorn, write to him that I love him?'

LEONATO This says she now, when she is beginning to write to him, for she'll be up twenty times a night, and there will she sit in her smock, till she have writ a sheet of paper. My daughter tells us all.

CLAUDIO Now you talk of a sheet of paper, I remember a pretty jest your daughter told us of.   140

LEONATO O when she had writ it and was reading it over, she found 'Benedick' and 'Beatrice' between the sheet?

CLAUDIO That.

LEONATO O, she tore the letter into a thousand halfpence, railed at herself, that she should be so immodest to write to one that she knew would flout

[149] my own spirit   *the way I feel*

[155] ecstasy   *frenzy*
[156] afeard   *afraid that*
[156-7] a desperate outrage   *something really violent*
[158] were   *would be*
[158-9] knew . . . other   *heard about it from someone else*
[159] discover it   *tell him (herself)*
[160-61] make but a sport of it   *only treat it as a joke*
[162] it were an alms   *it would be an act of charity*
[163-4] out . . . suspicion   *beyond any doubt*
[164] virtuous   *This, with* wise, *fulfils two of Benedick's own conditions for the 'ideal woman' (see back to l. 27-8).*
[167] blood   *passion*

[171] dotage   *excessive affection*
[172-3] daffed . . . myself   *laid aside all other considerations (like social inequality) and married her myself; Don Pedro aims to rouse Benedick's jealousy.*
[174] 'a   *he*
[175] Were . . . you   *do you really think it's a good idea*
[179-80] rather . . . crossness   *rather than give up any of her usual scorn (for* breath *and* words, *see II.1.245). This prepares for the fact that her* crossness *will continue!*

her. 'I measure him,' says she, 'by my own spirit; for
I should flout him if he writ to me – yea, though I
love him, I should.'   150

CLAUDIO Then down upon her knees she falls, weeps,
sobs, beats her heart, tears her hair, prays, curses, 'O
sweet Benedick – God give me patience!'

LEONATO She doth indeed, my daughter says so; and
the ecstasy hath so much overborne her that my
daughter is sometime afeard she will do a desperate
outrage to herself. It is very true.

DON PEDRO It were good that Benedick knew of it by
some other, if she will not discover it.

CLAUDIO To what end? He would make but a sport of   160
it and torment the poor lady worse.

DON PEDRO An he should, it were an alms to hang
him. She's an excellent sweet lady and, out of all
suspicion, she is virtuous.

CLAUDIO And she is exceeding wise.

DON PEDRO In everything but in loving Benedick.

LEONATO O my lord, wisdom and blood combating in
so tender a body, we have ten proofs to one that
blood hath the victory. I am sorry for her, as I have
just cause, being her uncle and her guardian.   170

DON PEDRO I would she had bestowed this dotage on
me; I would have daffed all other respects and
made her half myself. I pray you tell Benedick of it,
and hear what 'a will say.

LEONATO Were it good, think you?

CLAUDIO Hero thinks surely she will die; for she says
she will die if he love her not; and she will die ere she
make her love known; and she will die if he woo her
– rather than she will bate one breath of her
accustomed crossness.   180

[181] She doth well   *she's right*

make tender of   *offer*

[183] contemptible   *contemptuous*

[184] very proper   *fine*

[185–6] good outward happiness   *he certainly looks good; Don Pedro implies that appearances may not be everything*

[188–9] show . . . wit   *Another doubtful compliment; sparks suggests something very insubstantial, and even then only* like *wit.* wit: *intelligence*

[191] Hector   *The Trojan hero, who had at this time a reputation for being courageous but boastful.*

[193] with great discretion   *Implying he is a coward.*

[194] most Christian-like fear   *Christians were meant to avoid fighting, so this again implies that he is cowardly.*

[198] so will he do   *that's the way he does (enter a quarrel)*

[199–200] howsoever . . . make   *though you wouldn't think so from some of the profanities he utters*

[202–3] let . . . counsel   *let her get over it with sensible resolution*

[207] the while   *for the time being*

[208] modestly   *humbly*

[211] dinner   *Usually the midday meal and hence rather inconsistent with the time of this scene (evening at l. 38).*

DON PEDRO She doth well. If she should make tender
  of her love, 'tis very possible he'll scorn it, for the
  man – as you know all – hath a contemptible spirit.

CLAUDIO He is a very proper man.

DON PEDRO He hath indeed a good outward happiness.

CLAUDIO Before God, and in my mind, very wise.

DON PEDRO He doth indeed show some sparks that are
  like wit.

CLAUDIO And I take him to be valiant.   190

DON PEDRO As Hector, I assure you; and in the
  managing of quarrels you may say he is wise, for
  either he avoids them with great discretion, or
  undertakes them with a most Christian-like fear.

LEONATO If he do fear God, 'a must necessarily keep
  peace. If he break the peace, he ought to enter into a
  quarrel with fear and trembling.

DON PEDRO And so will he do, for the man doth fear
  God, howsoever it seems not in him by some large
  jests he will make. Well, I am sorry for your niece; 200
  shall we go seek Benedick, and tell him of her love?

CLAUDIO Never tell him, my lord; let her wear it out
  with good counsel.

LEONATO Nay, that's impossible; she may wear her
  heart out first.

DON PEDRO Well, we will hear further of it by your
  daughter. Let it cool the while, I love Benedick
  well, and I could wish he would modestly examine
  himself, to see how much he is unworthy so good a
  lady.   210

LEONATO My lord, will you walk? Dinner is ready.

[212] upon   *as a result of*

[212–13] I . . . expectation   *never again will I make predictions about what is going to happen*

[214] net   *Used to catch birds.*

[216] carry   *put into effect*

sport   *fun*

[217] and no such matter   *when there's nothing of the kind*

[218] would   *would like to*

[219] merely a dumb show   *just like a mime (for once, Beatrice and Benedick will be speechless!)*

[222] sadly borne   *conducted seriously*

[224] have their full bent   *are stretched to the limit (from archery, when the bow is ready to shoot)*

[225] it must be requited   *He now convinces himself that it is a matter of honour to return her love.*

censured   *criticised*

[229] I must not seem proud   *He uses their criticism as a means to revise his convictions; he doesn't question whether that criticism is fair.*

[230] their detractions   *the things said against them*

[232] I can . . . witness   *I can verify that*

[233] reprove   *deny*

[234–5] nor no . . . folly   *He decides to retract the idea that she is not wise to love him!*

[235] argument   *proof*

[236–7] odd quirks and remnants of wit   *He carefully minimises the potential ridicule in store for him if he changes his mind about love.* odd quirks: *irrelevant jibes*

[237] broken on   *Compare II.1.145.*

[238–40] But . . . age   *Another rationalisation; he can find reasons to support a change of heart, now that he wants to.*

[240] quips and sentences   *jokes and proverbial sayings*

[241–2] awe . . . humour   *frighten him from what he really wants*

They move out of BENEDICK's *hearing*

CLAUDIO If he do not dote on her upon this, I will
never trust my expectation.

DON PEDRO Let there be the same net spread for her,
and that must your daughter and her gentlewomen
carry. The sport will be when they hold one an
opinion of another's dotage, and no such matter;
that's the scene that I would see, which will be
merely a dumb show. Let us send her to call him in
to dinner.   220

       [*Exeunt* DON PEDRO, CLAUDIO, *and* LEONATO

BENEDICK [*Coming forward*] This can be no trick. The
conference was sadly borne. They have the truth of
this from Hero. They seem to pity the lady; it seems
her affections have their full bent. Love me? Why, it
must be requited! I hear how I am censured; they
say I will bear myself proudly if I perceive the love
come from her. They say, too, that she will rather
die than give any sign of affection. I did never think
to marry. I must not seem proud. Happy are they
that hear their detractions and can put them to   230
mending! They say the lady is fair – 'tis a truth, I
can bear them witness. And virtuous – 'tis so, I
cannot reprove it. And wise – but for loving me. By
my troth, it is no addition to her wit; nor no great
argument of her folly, for I will be horribly in love
with her. I may chance have some odd quirks and
remnants of wit broken on me because I have railed
so long against marriage. But doth not the appetite
alter? A man loves the meat in his youth that he
cannot endure in his age. Shall quips and sentences, 240
and these paper bullets of the brain, awe a man

[242-3] the world must be peopled   *His best reason yet!*

[244] I did ... live   *i.e. because of his career as a soldier; he is quickly modifying his earlier declarations.*

[246-7] I do ... her   *The eye begins to detect what the mind has been given to believe; another version of the* seeming truth.

[251-3] I took ... come   *Beatrice, in her 'accustomed crossness' (see l. 179), changes the meaning of* pains, *from trouble taken to actual pain.*

[254] You ... message   *He is trying to prise some indication of feeling from her.*

[255-6] just ... withal   *about as much pleasure as you can fit on the point of a knife and choke a jackdaw with. Not exactly encouraging for Benedick!*

[256-7] You have no stomach   *you've no appetite for (1) dinner or (2) conversation*

[264] a Jew   *Unhappily, this is equated with being mean. Jews were often characterised as misers due to their unpopular success as moneylenders.*

[265] picture   *portrait. He rushes off the stage, eager to comply with the conventional behaviour of the lover.*

from the career of his humour? No – the world must
be peopled. When I said I would die a bachelor, I
did not think I should live till I were married. Here
comes Beatrice.

Enter BEATRICE

By this day, she's a fair lady! I do spy some marks of
love in her.

BEATRICE Against my will I am sent to bid you come
in to dinner.

BENEDICK Fair Beatrice, I thank you for your pains. 250

BEATRICE I took no more pains for those thanks than
you take pains to thank me; if it had been painful I
would not have come.

BENEDICK You take pleasure, then, in the message?

BEATRICE Yea, just so much as you may take upon a
knife's point, and choke a daw withal. You have no
stomach, signor? Fare you well.

[*Exit*

BENEDICK Ha! 'Against my will I am sent to bid you
come in to dinner' – there's a double meaning in
that. 'I took no more pains for those thanks than 260
you took pains to thank me' – that's as much as to
say, 'Any pains that I take for you is as easy as
thanks.' If I do not take pity of her, I am a villain. If
I do not love her, I am a Jew. I will go get her
picture.

[*Exit*

ACT THREE, scene 1

The practice *continues, with Hero playing her part in effecting the change in Beatrice. This takes place in the same orchard and makes use of very similar tactics.*

[1] parlour   *A room adjoining the large hall.*

[3] Proposing   *in conversation*

[4] Ursley   *A familiar form of Ursula.*

[7] pleachèd bower   *This bower (formed by intertwining branches) would be the same as Benedick's arbour, which gives a neat theatrical unity to Don Pedro's schemes.*

[9–11] like . . . it   *A standard simile for something which is getting out of hand. (A weak monarch would show favour to some members of his court to gain support; they could then in effect control him.)*

[12] propose   *conversation*
office   *task*

[13] Bear . . . it   *carry it out properly*

[14] warrant   *assure*
presently   *immediately*

[16] trace . . . down   *walk backwards and forwards along this path*

[19] more . . . merit   *i.e. with great exaggeration. There seems to be more than a touch of Beatrice in her tone here.*

[21] matter   *substance*

[23] That . . . hearsay   *Their 'arrow' (see back to Don Pedro's claim at II.1.378), will be effective, even though it is only rumour – an apparent but not a proved truth.*

ACT THREE

Scene 1. *Enter* HERO, MARGARET and URSULA

HERO Good Margaret, run thee to the parlour;
      There shalt thou find my cousin Beatrice
      Proposing with the Prince and Claudio.
      Whisper her ear and tell her I and Ursley
      Walk in the orchard, and our whole discourse
      Is all of her. Say that thou overheardst us
      And bid her steal into the pleachèd bower,
      Where honeysuckles, ripened by the sun,
      Forbid the sun to enter – like favourites
      Made proud by princes, that advance their
         pride   10
      Against that power that bred it. There will she
        hide her
      To listen our propose. This is thy office;
      Bear thee well in it, and leave us alone.
MARGARET I'll make her come, I warrant you,
      presently.

[Exit

HERO Now, Ursula, when Beatrice doth come,
      As we do trace this alley up and down,
      Our talk must only be of Benedick.
      When I do name him, let it be thy part
      To praise him more than ever man did merit.
      My talk to thee must be how Benedick   20
      Is sick in love with Beatrice. Of this matter
      Is little Cupid's crafty arrow made,
      That only wounds by hearsay –

[24] lapwing *A bird which runs in a scuttling manner.*

[25] conference *talk*

[26] angling *fishing with rod and line (compare Claudio's comment at II.3.114)*

[26–8] The pleasant'st ... bait *An elegant image of fishing, which is then transferred to the real topic.*

[27] oars *i.e. fins*

[30] couchèd ... coverture *hidden in the shelter made by the honeysuckle*

[31] Fear ... dialogue *don't worry, I'll play my part all right*

[35] coy *shy*

[36] haggards of the rock *untrained female hawks*

[38] new-trothèd *newly-betrothed; a conveniently credible source of 'information'*

[42] To wish ... with *to urge him to struggle to subdue*

[44–6] Why ... upon *She takes up her cue as planned at l. 17. She is claiming that Benedick deserves as good a wife as Beatrice is ever likely to make. Two ideas are being telescoped in the use of* bed, *which starts as a synonym for wife – 'marriage-bed' – and then turns into a metaphor for her ability to fill the role.*

Enter BEATRICE, *behind*

Now begin;
For look where Beatrice like a lapwing runs
Close by the ground, to hear our conference.
URSULA [*Aside to* HERO] The pleasant'st angling is to
    see the fish
Cut with her golden oars the silver stream,
And greedily devour the treacherous bait;
So angle we for Beatrice, who even now
Is couchèd in the woodbine coverture.   30
Fear you not my part of the dialogue.
HERO [*Aside*] Then go we near her, that her ear lose
    nothing
Of the false sweet bait that we lay for it.

They approach the bower

[*Aloud*] No truly, Ursula, she is too disdainful;
I know her spirits are as coy and wild
As haggards of the rock.
URSULA   But are you sure
That Benedick loves Beatrice so entirely?
HERO So says the Prince, and my new-trothèd lord.
URSULA And did they bid you tell her of it, madam?
HERO They did entreat me to acquaint her of it;   40
But I persuaded them, if they loved Benedick,
To wish him wrestle with affection
And never to let Beatrice know of it.
URSULA Why did you so? Doth not the gentleman
Deserve as full as fortunate a bed

[48] as much . . . yielded *The line allows three levels of meaning:
(1) for Beatrice's ears, the straight exaggeration – as much as it is possible
to give; (2) moral – as much as it is permissible to give, and (3) nicely
sceptical – as much as it is wise to give!*

[50] of prouder stuff *of a more arrogant disposition (Benedick was
also accused of being proud, II.3.185).*

[51] Disdain . . . eyes *While this criticises, it also manages to convey
some of Beatrice's attractiveness!*

[52] Misprising *despising (literally: undervaluing)*

[54] All . . . weak *everything else seems inferior to her (because she's
so sure of the value of her own intelligence)*

She cannot love *Hero is suggesting this as a serious deficiency.*

[55] Nor ... affection *or even to pretend to care or entertain the idea
of caring (for anyone else)*

[56] so self-endeared *so fond of herself*

[58] make sport at it *Compare Claudio about Benedick II.3.161.*

[60] how rarely *however finely*

[61] But . . . backward *turn (his good points) upside down*

[62] sister *Implying effeminacy.*

[63] black *dark-skinned (as opposed to fair-faced)*

[63-4] drawing . . . blot *while designing a grotesque figure made an
ugly blot*

[64] ill-headed *with a bad point*

[65] low *short*

an . . . cut *a roughly-cut agate. Agate was used to make seals, in which
designs were carved.*

[66] vane *weather-cock; the comparison implies someone talking
inconsistently*

[67] a block movèd with none *i.e. totally solid. Hero's examples,
while proving to Beatrice that she is far too critical, in fact give us more proof
of her wit.*

[69-70] And . . . purchaseth *i.e. she never commends anything for
its real value*

[71] carping *This puts Beatrice's witty comments in a new
perspective!*

[72] not *A superfluous negative.*

from all fashions *against all conventions*

As ever Beatrice shall couch upon?
HERO O god of love! I know he doth deserve
 As much as may be yielded to a man.
 But Nature never framed a woman's heart
 Of prouder stuff than that of Beatrice.   50
 Disdain and scorn ride sparkling in her eyes,
 Misprising what they look on; and her wit
 Values itself so highly, that to her
 All matter else seems weak. She cannot love,
 Nor take no shape nor project of affection,
 She is so self-endeared.
URSULA   Sure I think so;
 And therefore certainly it were not good
 She knew his love, lest she'll make sport at it.
HERO Why, you speak truth. I never yet saw man,
 How wise, how noble, young, how rarely
  featured,   60
 But she would spell him backward. If fair-
  faced,
 She would swear the gentleman should be her
  sister;
 If black, why Nature, drawing of an antic,
 Made a foul blot; if tall, a lance ill-headed;
 If low, an agate very vilely cut;
 If speaking, why, a vane blown with all winds;
 If silent, why, a block movèd with none;
 So turns she every man the wrong side out,
 And never gives to truth and virtue that
 Which simpleness and merit purchaseth.   70
URSULA Sure, sure, such carping is not
  commendable.
HERO No, not to be so odd and from all fashions
 As Beatrice is, cannot be commendable.

[76] Out of myself   *away from my intention*
press . . . wit   *She implies that Beatrice would overdo it (metaphor drawn from a form of torture).*

[77] like covered fire   *i.e. smothering his passion*

[79] die with mocks   *be killed by ridicule*

[83] counsel   *advise*

[84–5] I'll . . . with   *She plans some mild slanders to reduce Benedick's opinion of Beatrice. Coming from Hero, about whom serious slanders are planned, this is of course horribly ironical.*

[85–6] One . . . liking   *it's extraordinary how much damage to affection such criticism can do*

[90] prized to have   *thought to have, and valued for – with an underlying hint that such a reputation may not be justified (something that Beatrice will then be anxious to prove)*

[91] rare   *fine*

[92] He . . . Italy   *i.e. he's really outstanding*

[95] Speaking my fancy   *saying what I think*

[96] argument   *intelligent conversation*

[97] Goes foremost in report   *is most highly thought of*

[98] name   *reputation (she can't of course concede that he excels Claudio)*

[99] His . . . it   *She's sticking to her point – Benedick does not have a mere name, he has fully earned it.*

[101] every day tomorrow   *(1) from tomorrow, everyday; (2) it's always tomorrow (never today); compare Claudio at II.1.350.*

[102] attires   *head-dresses*

[103] furnish   *adorn*

But who dare tell her so? If I should speak
She would mock me into air; O, she would
    laugh me
Out of myself, press me to death with wit.
Therefore let Benedick, like covered fire,
Consume away in sighs, waste inwardly.
It were a better death than die with mocks,
Which is as bad as die with tickling.   80

URSULA Yet tell her of it; hear what she will say.

HERO No; rather I will go to Benedick
And counsel him to fight against his passion.
And truly, I'll devise some honest slanders
To stain my cousin with. One doth not know
How much an ill word may empoison liking.

URSULA O, do not do your cousin such a wrong!
She cannot be so much without true
    judgement –
Having so swift and excellent a wit
As she is prized to have – as to refuse   90
So rare a gentleman as Signor Benedick.

HERO He is the only man in Italy,
Always excepted my dear Claudio.

URSULA I pray you be not angry with me, madam,
Speaking my fancy: Signor Benedick
For shape, for bearing, argument and valour,
Goes foremost in report through Italy.

HERO Indeed he hath an excellent good name.

URSULA His excellence did earn it, ere he had it.
When are you married, madam?   100

HERO Why, every day tomorrow. Come, go in.
I'll show thee some attires, and have thy
    counsel
Which is the best to furnish me tomorrow.

[104] limed   *as a bird in bird-lime*

[105] haps   *chance*

[106] traps   *This picks up Ursula's use of limed as well as referring to the whole scheme; a saying truer than she realises.*

[107–16] What fire ... reportingly   *This speech is formally organised in rhyming quatrains and a couplet like a shortened sonnet. The form echoes the more conventional attitudes indicated in the content.*

[107] fire   *(1) her ears are burning, from having been talked about (2) what she has heard has aroused passion*

[109] Contempt, farewell   *Beatrice is even quicker than Benedick to revise her attitudes!*

[110] No ... such   *there's no advantage in hiding behind these*

[112] Taming ... hand   *A perfect line, to convey a genuine acceptance of love and her intention to conform. It also rounds off the scene by developing the image of 'haggards of the rock' that Hero has used at l. 36.*

[113] incite   *encourage*

[114] bind our loves up   *(1) in the formal bond (2) come together, intertwine*

holy band   *marriage, or the ring which symbolises it*

[115–16] and I ... reportingly   *and I know it to be true myself (and not just from what is said)*

ACT THREE, scene 2

With Beatrice's reference to marriage (at the end of III.1) and Benedick being teased for his love-symptoms, this match is nearly secured; just as the overshadowing threat to the other match grows into a reality – a scene carefully poised between imminent success and imminent disaster. It takes place inside Leonato's house.

[2] consummate   *i.e. all the ceremonies completed*

[3] bring   *accompany*

[4] vouchsafe   *allow*

[5–6] as great ... gloss   *He doesn't want to tarnish Claudio's newly-wedded happiness. Also an undercurrent of dramatic irony: soil was often used of moral stain, and gloss implies superficial lustre.*

[7–8] only ... company   *require only Benedick to accompany me*

[9] he is all mirth   *Don Pedro knows that after II.3. this is no longer the case.*

They move out of BEATRICE's *hearing*

URSULA She's limed, I warrant you; we have caught
  her, madam!
HERO If it prove so, then loving goes by haps.
  Some Cupid kills with arrows, some with traps.
         [*Exeunt* HERO *and* URSULA
BEATRICE [*Coming forward*] What fire is in mine
  ears? Can this be true?
  Stand I condemned for pride and scorn so
  much?
  Contempt, farewell! And maiden pride, adieu!
  No glory lives behind the back of such.   110
  And, Benedick, love on; I will requite thee,
  Taming my wild heart to thy loving hand.
  If thou dost love, my kindness shall incite thee
  To bind our loves up in a holy band;
  For others say thou dost deserve, and I
  Believe it better than reportingly.
            [*Exit

Scene 2. *Enter* DON PEDRO, CLAUDIO, BENEDICK *and*
LEONATO

DON PEDRO I do but stay till your marriage be
 consummate, and then go I toward Arragon.
CLAUDIO I'll bring you thither, my lord, if you'll
 vouchsafe me.
DON PEDRO Nay, that would as great a soil in the new
 gloss of your marriage, as to show a child his new
 coat and forbid him to wear it. I will only be bold
 with Benedick for his company; for, from the crown
 of his head to the sole of his foot, he is all mirth. He

[10] cut Cupid's bowstring *i.e. averted falling in love (perhaps suggesting jilting)*

[11] hangman *rascal*

dare not shoot *Although they dare, in Cupid's place – see II.1.379.*

[12] clapper *the bell's tongue*

[14] Gallants *gentlemen*

[15] sadder *more serious*

[16] hope *think*

[17] truant *turn-coat*

[17–18] There's ... love *i.e. he isn't capable (of real feeling). For blood as representing emotion, see II.3.167.*

[20] I have the toothache *Benedick is covering his face to hide his lack of beard.*

[21] Draw it *pull it out*

[23] You ... afterwards *Claudio takes him literally; the tooth has to be tied before it can be pulled. From execution, where people were hung, drawn and quartered.*

[26] a humour or a worm *Both were considered possible causes for tooth decay (for humour, see note at I.1.129).*

[27–8] everyone ... it *other people can always get over a pain they aren't experiencing; a sarcastic version of the maxim used by Leonato at V.1.36–7.*

[29] Yet say I *I still say*

[30–5] There ... doublet *Reference to the varied fashion of the day; Benedick the lover has taken a sudden interest in his clothes (compare Claudio, II.3.18). Fashion is also a metaphor for the theme of appearances.*

[30] fancy *love*

[31] a fancy *liking or affectation*

[34] slops *loose breeches*

[36] this foolery *i.e. the dictates of fashion*

[37] no fool for fancy *not under the dictates of love*

[40] old signs *the familiar marks*

'A *he*

'a *in the*

[41] bode *mean*

hath twice or thrice cut Cupid's bowstring, and the 10
little hangman dare not shoot at him; he hath a
heart as sound as a bell and his tongue is the clapper
– for what his heart thinks, his tongue speaks.

BENEDICK Gallants, I am not as I have been.

LEONATO So say I – methinks you are sadder.

CLAUDIO I hope he be in love.

DON PEDRO Hang him, truant! There's no true drop of
blood in him to be truly touched with love. If he be
sad, he wants money.

BENEDICK I have the toothache. 20

DON PEDRO Draw it.

BENEDICK Hang it!

CLAUDIO You must hang it first, and draw it afterwards.

DON PEDRO What – sigh for the toothache?

LEONATO Where is but a humour or a worm.

BENEDICK Well, everyone can master a grief but he
that has it.

CLAUDIO Yet say I, he is in love.

DON PEDRO There is no appearance of fancy in him, 30
unless it be a fancy that he hath to strange disguises,
as to be a Dutchman today, a Frenchman tomorrow, or in the shape of two countries at once, as a
German from the waist downward, all slops, and a
Spaniard from the hip upward, no doublet. Unless
he have a fancy to this foolery, as it appears he hath,
he is no fool for fancy, as you would have it appear
he is.

CLAUDIO If he be not in love with some woman, there
is no believing old signs. 'A brushes his hat 'a 40
mornings – what should that bode?

DON PEDRO Hath any man seen him at the barber's?

[44] old ornament of his cheek   *i.e. his beard. Beatrice announced her dislike of beards at II.1.30. (The fate of his beard is less than dignified though perfectly normal at that time!)*

[48] civet   *A popular perfume of the day and the base of many modern perfumes (from the civet cat).*

[52] note   *indication*
melancholy   *The traditional aspect of the lover.*

[54] paint himself   *use make-up*

[54–5] For . . . him   *and I've heard the way that's talked about*

[56] but   *but what about*

[56–7] which . . . stops   *now that he's turned lover, he's more interested in love-songs; governed by stops: ruled by the frets on the lute*

[58] for   *about*

[61] would I   *I'd like to*

[61–2] one that knows him not   *The play on know (know his character and know him sexually) sets off the bawdy punning of the next two lines.*

[63] ill conditions   *bad points*

[63–4] in despite of all   *regardless of everything*

[64] dies   *(1) wastes away (2) a common metaphor for sexual orgasm.*

[65] buried with her face upwards   *Either under the ground, or under Benedick.*

[66] charm   *cure. Charms are verbal sequences repeated to effect a cure.*

[67] studied   *learnt by heart*

[68–9] hobby-horses   *buffoons*

[Exeunt]   *Benedick, seeking discussion to secure one match, leaves Don John his opportunity to begin the destruction of the other.*

[70] For my life   *I'll swear (this will be)*

[72] 'Tis even so   *that's it*

Margaret   *Probably meant to be Ursula, though they are both involved.*

[73] parts   *i.e. in the practice*

CLAUDIO No, but the barber's man hath been seen with him, and the old ornament of his cheek hath already stuffed tennis balls.

LEONATO Indeed he looks younger than he did, by the loss of a beard.

DON PEDRO Nay, 'a rubs himself with civet; can you smell him out by that?

CLAUDIO That's as much as to say the sweet youth's in love. 50

DON PEDRO The greatest note of it is his melancholy.

CLAUDIO And when was he wont to wash his face?

DON PEDRO Yea, or to paint himself? For the which, I hear what they say of him.

CLAUDIO Nay, but his jesting spirit, which is now crept into a lute string and now governed by stops?

DON PEDRO Indeed, that tells a heavy tale for him. Conclude, conclude – he is in love.

CLAUDIO Nay, but I know who loves him. 60

DON PEDRO That would I know too; I warrant one that knows him not.

CLAUDIO Yes, and his ill conditions, and in despite of all, dies for him.

DON PEDRO She shall be buried with her face upwards.

BENEDICK Yet is this no charm for the toothache. Old signor, walk aside with me: I have studied eight or nine wise words to speak to you which these hobbyhorses must not hear.

[*Exeunt* BENEDICK *and* LEONATO

DON PEDRO For my life, to break with him about 70 Beatrice.

CLAUDIO 'Tis even so; Hero and Margaret have by this played their parts with Beatrice; and then the two bears will not bite one another when they meet.

[76] Good den *Shortened form of 'God give you good evening'.*
[77] If . . . served *if you've time*
[83] Means *intends*

[88] any impediment *anything to stop it (the word used in the calling of marriage banns)*

[88–9] I pray . . . it *for goodness' sake reveal it (Claudio might well be impatient at Don John's tactics)*

[90–5] You may . . . ill-bestowed *His whole speech is characterised by its staccato quality; either he is nervous in his part, or he is pretending to be anxious. He is not in any case known for linguistic ease – see Introduction, p. 18.*

[90–1] let that appear hereafter *that remains to be seen (a strong irony)*

[91] aim better at me *judge me more accurately; a metaphor from archery*

[92] manifest *show*

[92–3] holds you well *thinks highly of you; this recalls one of the main causes of Don John's envy – see I.3.64.*

[93] holp *helped*

[94–5] suit . . . ill-bestowed *a thorough waste of time and effort*

[97–8] circumstances shortened *i.e. to cut a long story short*

[98] she . . . of *she's been the topic of conversation for too long*

[99] disloyal *unfaithful*

[101] Leonato's . . . Hero *After the evasive build-up, a starkly dramatic revelation in a sneering tone.*

[104] paint out *show fully*

[105] I could say she were worse *I could easily use a worse word*

Enter DON JOHN

DON JOHN My lord and brother, God save you!

DON PEDRO Good den, brother.

DON JOHN If your leisure served, I would speak with you.

DON PEDRO In private?

DON JOHN If it please you. Yet Count Claudio may 80
hear, for what I would speak of concerns him.

DON PEDRO What's the matter?

DON JOHN [*To* CLAUDIO] Means your lordship to be married tomorrow?

DON PEDRO You know he does.

DON JOHN I know not that, when he knows what I know.

CLAUDIO If there be any impediment I pray you discover it.

DON JOHN You may think I love you not; let that 90
appear hereafter, and aim better at me by that I now will manifest. For my brother – I think he holds you well and in dearness of heart – hath holp to effect your ensuing marriage: surely suit ill-spent and labour ill-bestowed!

DON PEDRO Why, what's the matter?

DON JOHN I came hither to tell you, and circumstances shortened – for she has been too long a-talking of – the lady is disloyal.

CLAUDIO Who – Hero? 100

DON JOHN: Even she. Leonato's Hero; your Hero; every man's Hero.

CLAUDIO Disloyal?

DON JOHN The word is too good to paint out her wickedness. I could say she were worse – think you

[106] fit her to it   *show you how it's applicable*

[107] warrant   *proof*

[108–9] even . . . wedding-day   *This is carefully emphasised.*

[109] then   *still (after seeing that)*

[110–111] fit your honour   *be more suitable for one of your position (or integrity)*

[112] May . . . so   *can this be true*

[113] I will not think it   *I won't believe it (Is there any contrast in their reactions?)*

[114–15] If . . . know   *Don John asserts that if you can't believe what you see, you can't believe anything; false reasoning, which they fail to detect. His whole plan depends precisely on the deceptive nature of appearances, the* seeming *truth.*

[116] enough   *i.e. to convince you*

[119–20] in . . . her   *Claudio (a renowned soldier—see I.1.13) is quick to plan retaliation. Is such a revenge justifiable?*

[124] Bear it coldly but till   *stay calm just until*

[125] issue   *outcome (compare II.2.51)*

[126] untowardly turned   *wretchedly changed*

[127] mischief   *evil*

thwarting   *frustrating*

[128] O plague . . . prevented   *Don John's rejoinder is exultant compared with the bewilderment of the others. The contrast is highlighted by the use of the same syntactic structure for each comment.*

[129] the sequel   *what follows; i.e. the 'evidence' for the eyes.*

ACT THREE, scene 3

In this (the play's central scene) the main plots are suddenly suspended while we encounter for the first time a lower social level. Initially it appears to be a comic digression, but Shakespeare is working his own practice in this; the least significant suddenly becomes the most important – a promise of an eventual solution to counter-balance the evil in progress. The scene takes place on the street outside Leonato's house.

DOGBERRY, VERGES   *Both names suggest physical types; Dogberry, the fruit of the dogwood, round and red; and Verges possibly from verge, a rod of office, and therefore long and thin.*

of a worse title, and I will fit her to it. Wonder not till further warrant. Go but with me tonight, you shall see her chamber window entered, even the night before her wedding day. If you love her then, tomorrow wed her; but it would better fit your 110 honour to change your mind.

CLAUDIO May this be so?

DON PEDRO I will not think it.

DON JOHN If you dare not trust that you see, confess not that you know. If you will follow me, I will show you enough; and when you have seen more and heard more, proceed accordingly.

CLAUDIO If I see anything tonight why I should not marry her tomorrow, in the congregation where I should wed, there will I shame her.   120

DON PEDRO And as I wooed for thee to obtain her, I will join with thee to disgrace her.

DON JOHN I will disparage her no farther till you are my witnesses. Bear it coldly but till midnight, and let the issue show itself.

DON PEDRO O day untowardly turned!

CLAUDIO O mischief strangely thwarting!

DON JOHN O plague right well prevented! So will you say when you have seen the sequel.

[*Exeunt*

Scene 3. *Enter* DOGBERRY, VERGES, *with the* WATCH

DOGBERRY Are you good men and true?

VERGES Yea, or else it were pity but they should suffer salvation, body and soul.

DOGBERRY Nay, that were a punishment too good for them, if they should have any allegiance in them,

the WATCH   *The men who patrolled the streets of Elizabethan towns at night, to maintain law and order. They had none of the professional training of a modern police force, and so they were a frequent target for ridicule.*

[1] good men and true   *A standard form of address.*

[2] or else ... should   *if not, it's a pity for they will*

[3] salvation   *(for damnation – the first of many words used wrongly by them)*

[5] any allegiance   *(for lack of allegiance)*

[7] give them their charge   *tell them what their duties are*

[9] desartless   *without merit (for most deserving)*

[10] constable   *the man in charge*

[11] Oatcake; Seacoal   *Homely names, indicating the low social status but solid worthiness.*

[14] a good name   *Presumably because coal was valuable.*

[14–15] well-favoured   *good-looking (for favoured, in the sense of being blessed)*

[15] the gift of fortune   *good luck (from fortunate circumstances)*

[16] by nature   *inherent ability; Dogberry uses the much-debated contrast between Fortune and Nature, but has, characteristically, applied them the wrong way round.*

[19] favour   *looks*

[23] senseless   *(for sensible)*

[25] comprehend   *(for apprehend)*

vagrom   *(for vagrant)*

[26] bid any man stand   *order anyone to halt*

[127]'a   *he*

[28] take no note of him   *ignore him (marvellous advice from the law-keeper). Here and elsewhere Dogberry confuses advice on the duty of the Watch with advice he would give for personal behaviour.*

[29] presently   *immediately*

[31–2] is none   *isn't one*

[33–4] True ... subjects   *i.e. they can leave all criminals alone!*

[35] for   *because*

[36] tolerable   *(for intolerable)*

[37–8] We ... watch   *Unconsciously satirical, and doubtless greatly appreciated by a contemporary audience.*

being chosen for the Prince's watch.

VERGES Well, give them their charge, neighbour Dogberry.

DOGBERRY First, who think you the most desartless man to be constable? 10

FIRST WATCH Hugh Oatcake, sir, or George Seacoal, for they can write and read.

DOGBERRY Come hither, neighbour Seacoal; God hath blessed you with a good name. To be a well-favoured man is the gift of fortune, but to write and read comes by nature.

SECOND WATCH Both which, Master Constable –

DOGBERRY You have. I knew it would be your answer. Well, for your favour, sir, why, give God thanks and make no boast of it; and for your writing 20 and reading, let that appear when there is no need of such vanity. You are thought here to be the most senseless and fit man for the constable of the Watch; therefore, bear you the lantern. This is your charge: you shall comprehend all vagrom men; you are to bid any man stand, in the Prince's name.

SECOND WATCH How if 'a will not stand?

DOGBERRY Why then, take no note of him, but let him go; and presently call the rest of the watch together and thank God you are rid of a knave. 30

VERGES If he will not stand when he is bidden, he is none of the Prince's subjects.

DOGBERRY True, and they are to meddle with none but the Prince's subjects. You shall also make no noise in the streets; for, for the watch to babble and to talk is most tolerable and not to be endured.

SECOND WATCH We will rather sleep than talk; we know what belongs to a watch.

[39] ancient *experienced*

[41-2] have . . . stolen *A nice irony.*

[41] bills *The Watch's weapons, like battleaxes with long shafts.*

[45-6] let . . . sober *In which case they won't need any attention.*

[51] no true man *not honest*

[51-3] and for . . . honesty *Dogberry again confuses duty with personal conduct. He places great emphasis on* honesty *as a virtue.*

[54-5] If . . . him *The First Watch asks the relevant question!*

[56-60] Truly . . . company *Again the confusion; he quotes the proverb to advise against meddling.*

[59] steal *creep (he is probably unaware of the pun he has made)*

[63] by my will *of my own accord*

[64] much more *(for* much less*)*

[70-2] for . . . bleats *In his analogy, he again shows the Watch to be useless; if the nurse can't hear her own charge crying, she will hardly hear the Watch (a calf) calling to her.*

DOGBERRY Why, you speak like an ancient and most quiet watchman, for I cannot see how sleeping 40 should offend; only, have a care that your bills be not stolen. Well, you are to call at all the alehouses and bid those that are drunk get them to bed.

FIRST WATCH How if they will not?

DOGBERRY Why, then let them alone till they are sober. If they make you not then the better answer, you may say they are not the men you took them for.

FIRST WATCH Well, sir.

DOGBERRY If you meet a thief you may suspect him, 50 by virtue of your office, to be no true man; and for such kind of men, the less you meddle or make with them, why, the more is for your honesty.

FIRST WATCH If we know him to be a thief, shall we not lay hands on him?

DOGBERRY Truly, by your office you may, but I think they that touch pitch will be defiled. The most peaceable way for you, if you do take a thief, is to let him show himself what he is and steal out of your company. 60

VERGES You have been always called a merciful man, partner.

DOGBERRY Truly, I would not hang a dog by my will, much more a man who hath any honesty in him.

VERGES If you hear a child cry in the night, you must call to the nurse and bid her still it.

SECOND WATCH How if the nurse be asleep and will not hear us?

DOGBERRY Why then, depart in peace and let the child wake her with crying; for the ewe that will not 70 hear her lamb when it baes will never answer a calf

[75] present   *(for* represent*)*

[76] stay   *stop*

[77] by'r lady   *by our Lady*

'a   *he*

[79] statutes   *laws*

[79–80] Marry . . . willing   *Dogberry quickly modifies his view, in order to win the bet.*

[81] an offence   *(for* offensive*)*

[81–2] it . . . will   *By this generalisation he renders the Watch powerless.*

[84] Ha, ah ha   *He is crowing with triumph rather than laughing.*

[85] of weight chances   *of importance happens*

[86] Keep . . . own   *This is similar to the advice that was given to juries.*

[87] Come, neighbour   *(They start to leave the stage.)*

[94] coil   *commotion*

[95] be vigitant   *(for* be vigilant*)*

[96] What   *An exploratory greeting, like 'Is that you?'*

[97] Peace, stir not   *quiet, don't move*

[100] Mass   *by the Mass (a common oath)*

my elbow itched   *Thought to indicate that someone was near.*

[101] scab   *(1) as a result of the itching (2) a contemptible person*

when he bleats.

VERGES 'Tis very true.

DOGBERRY This is the end of the charge: you, constable, are to present the Prince's own person. If you meet the Prince in the night, you may stay him.

VERGES Nay, by'r lady, that I think 'a cannot.

DOGBERRY Five shillings to one on't, with any man that knows the statutes, he may stay him. Marry, not without the Prince be willing, for indeed the   80 watch ought to offend no man, and it is an offence to stay a man against his will.

VERGES By'r lady, I think it be so.

DOGBERRY Ha, ah ha! Well, masters, good-night; an there be any matter of weight chances, call up me. Keep your fellows' counsels and your own, and good-night. Come, neighbour.

SECOND WATCH Well, masters, we hear our charge. Let us go sit here upon the church bench till two, and then all to bed.   90

DOGBERRY [*Coming back*] One word more, honest neighbours: I pray you watch about Signor Leonato's door, for the wedding being there tomorrow, there is a great coil tonight. Adieu. Be vigitant, I beseech you.

                        [*Exeunt* DOGBERRY *and* VERGES

Enter BORACHIO *and* CONRADE

BORACHIO What, Conrade?

SECOND WATCH [*Aside*] Peace; stir not.

BORACHIO Conrade, I say!

CONRADE Here, man, I am at thy elbow.

BORACHIO Mass, and my elbow itched; I thought   100 there would a scab follow.

[102] I will . . . that *I'll pay you back later*

[103] forward *get on*

[104] penthouse *overhanging roof*

[105–6] like a true drunkard *He is going to play the drunkard – not difficult as he is clearly fairly drunk already!*

[107–8] yet stand close *stay hidden still*

[112] dear *(1) costly (2) precious (to anyone)*

[115–16] may make what price they will *can ask any price they want*

[117] I wonder at it *it's amazing*

[118] unconfirmed *inexperienced (with a pun in connection with wonder since they are both religious terms)*

[120] is nothing to a man *shows nothing about him (i.e. Don John may appear well-born, but that doesn't prove anything)*

[121] apparel *clothes*

[124] Tush *Rubbish!*

[125] But see'st thou not *Borachio is determined to comment on the deceptive effects of fashion. His examples at l. 132 ff. are all reductive.*

[127] that Deformed *Picking up the word thief, the Second Watch pretends to know his identity.*

[129] like *pretending to be*

[131] vane *weather vane (which might creak as it turned)*

[133] how giddily 'a turns about *i.e. similar to the weather vane*

CONRADE I will owe thee an answer for that; and now
forward with thy tale.

BORACHIO Stand thee close then under this penthouse, for it drizzles rain, and I will, like a true
drunkard, utter all to thee.

SECOND WATCH [*Aside*] Some treason, masters; yet
stand close.

BORACHIO Therefore know, I have earned of Don
John a thousand ducats.   110

CONRADE Is it possible that any villainy should be so
dear?

BORACHIO Thou shouldst rather ask if it were possible
any villainy should be so rich; for when rich villains
have need of poor ones, poor ones may make what
price they will.

CONRADE I wonder at it.

BORACHIO That shows thou art unconfirmed; thou
knowest that the fashion of a doublet, or a hat, or a
cloak, is nothing to a man.   120

CONRADE Yes, it is apparel.

BORACHIO I mean the fashion.

CONRADE Yes, the fashion is the fashion.

BORACHIO Tush! I may as well say the fool's the fool.
But see'st thou not what a deformed thief this
fashion is?

SECOND WATCH [*Aside*] I know that Deformed; 'a has
been a vile thief this seven year; 'a goes up and
down like a gentleman. I remember his name.

BORACHIO Didst thou not hear somebody?   130

CONRADE No, 'twas the vane on the house.

BORACHIO Seest thou not, I say, what a deformed thief
this fashion is? How giddily 'a turns about all the

[134] hot-bloods *young men*

[135] fashioning them like *turning them into*

[135–6] like . . . painting *Presumably referring to a particular painting.*

[136] reechy *discoloured, perhaps by smoke*

[136–7] like god Bel's priests *A reference to a story in the Apocrypha.*

[137–8] the shaven Hercules *A rather mixed allusion to the story of Hercules' humiliation, when he was dressed as a woman and made to perform menial tasks (compare II.1.249).*

[138] smirched *dirtied*

[139] cod-piece *the often decorative pouch at the front of a man's breeches (This Hercules is clearly in Elizabethan costume.)*

massy *massive*

[141–2] the fashion . . . man *it's fashion and not over-wearing that makes the life of clothes short*

[143] giddy with the fashion too *Conrade is criticising Borachio's long digression; giddy no doubt implies his inebriation.*

[148] leans me out *me is for emphasis, like 'would you believe'*

[150] I tell this tale vilely *In his state he can't organise the report as clearly as he might!*

[152] possessed *informed; with the suitable implication of being taken over by a devil (i.e. Don John, see l. 157)*

[154] amiable *amorous; stronger than the modern meaning of friendly.*

[162] enraged *passionate; through anger now, rather than love.*

[163] temple *church*

[165] o'er *over*

hot-bloods, between fourteen and five-and-thirty –
sometimes fashioning them like Pharaoh's soldiers
in the reechy painting, sometime like god Bel's
priests in the old church window, sometime like the
shaven Hercules in the smirched worm-eaten
tapestry, where his cod-piece seems as massy as his
club?   140

CONRADE All this I see, and I see that the fashion
wears out more apparel than the man. But art not
thou thyself giddy with the fashion too, that thou
hast shifted out of thy tale into telling me of the
fashion?

BORACHIO Not so, neither; but know that I have
tonight wooed Margaret, the Lady Hero's gentlewoman, by the name of Hero. She leans me out at
her mistress' chamber window, bids me a thousand
times good-night – I tell this tale vilely – I should 150
first tell thee how the Prince, Claudio, and my
master, planted and placed and possessed by my
master, Don John, saw afar off in the orchard this
amiable encounter.

CONRADE And thought they Margaret was Hero?

BORACHIO Two of them did, the Prince and Claudio;
but the devil my master knew she was Margaret;
and partly by his oaths, which first possessed them,
partly by the dark night, which did deceive them,
but chiefly by my villainy, which did confirm any 160
slander that Don John had made, away went
Claudio enraged – swore he would meet her as he
was appointed next morning at the temple; and
there, before the whole congregation, shame her
with what he saw o'er night, and send her home
again without a husband.

[168] stand   *halt*
[170] recovered   *(for* discovered*)*
[171] lechery   *(for* treachery*)*
[173] I know him   *He builds up his claim (see back to l. 127).*
'a   *he*
a lock   *a fashionable curl hanging by the ear*
[175] made bring   *made to bring*
[178–9] let us obey you   *(for* let us order you*)*
[180] a goodly commodity   *(1) useful to them (2) fine merchandise (he is punning on* charge *and* bills *as bonds of sale.)*
[181] taken up   *(1) arrested (2) bought on credit*
[182] in question   *(1) likely to be questioned (2) in demand; and perhaps (3) of questionable value*

ACT THREE, scene 4

Back inside the house Hero's wedding preparations continue, with III.2 providing a perspective for dramatic irony. Despite the arrest, there can as yet be no confidence that the Watch will act competently, and so a tension is maintained between the light surface of the scene and the underlying fears for its outcome. For Beatrice, the scene is a parallel to the teasing of Benedick at III.2.

[2] desire   *ask*
[5] Well   *right away*
[6] rebato   *a stiff ornamental collar*
[9] 's   *it's*

The WATCH *come forward excitedly*

SECOND WATCH We charge you in the Prince's name, stand!

FIRST WATCH Call up the right Master Constable. We have here recovered the most dangerous piece of 170 lechery that ever was known in the commonwealth.

SECOND WATCH And one Deformed is one of them; I know him, 'a wears a lock.

CONRADE Masters, masters –

FIRST WATCH You'll be made bring Deformed forth, I warrant you.

CONRADE Masters –

SECOND WATCH Never speak, we charge you; let us obey you to go with us.

BORACHIO We are like to prove a goodly commodity, 180 being taken up of these men's bills.

CONRADE A commodity in question, I warrant you. Come, we'll obey you.

[*Exeunt*

Scene 4. *Enter* HERO *with* MARGARET *and* URSULA

HERO Good Ursula, wake my cousin Beatrice and desire her to rise.

URSULA I will, lady.

HERO And bid her come hither.

URSULA Well.

[*Exit*

MARGARET Troth, I think your other rebato were better.

HERO No, pray thee good Meg, I'll wear this.

MARGARET By my troth, 's not so good; and I warrant your cousin will say so. 10

137

[13] new tire   *new head-dress (not seen on stage)*

[14] a thought   *a shade*

[15] a most rare fashion   *very fine indeed*

[17] that exceeds   *that's better than anything*

[18] night-gown   *The equivalent of a modern dressing gown.*

[19] cuts   *slits in the dress, to show different coloured material underneath*

[20] down-sleeves   *loose open sleeves (ornamental)*

[21] round underborne   *trimmed all round the hem*

tinsel   *A sparkling silk fabric interwoven with gold or silver thread.*

[22] quaint   *elegant*

[23] on 't   *of it*

[24–5] for . . . heavy   *As though with premonition of the coming disaster.*

[26] soon   *i.e. as soon as you are married; Margaret is making a suggestive pun, perhaps to cheer Hero up.*

[28] Fie . . . ashamed   *There·are two possible tones for this; she might be seriously indignant, now that she is facing the 'reality' of marriage as opposed to the fictions of courtship; but it is more in character (see II.1; III.1. and later this scene) if she is mockingly shocked.*

[29] honourably   *legitimately (because she has referred to her husband-to-be)*

[30] Is . . . beggar   *i.e. isn't marriage always legitimate*

[31] honourable without marriage   *a man of honour without having to be married to prove it*

[31–3] I think . . . husband   *you'd have preferred it if I had said, 'by the weight of a husband' (She is teasing Hero, ignoring the fact that her 'objection' is to the whole comment, not just to man.)*

[33] an   *if*

wrest   *twist*

[35] the heavier for a husband   *She revises her original line.*

[35–6] an it . . . wife   *so long as they are married to one another*

[57] light   *wanton (because adulterous)*

else   *if you don't believe me*

[39] coz   *An affectionate version of cousin.*

HERO My cousin's a fool, and thou art another. I'll
wear none but this.

MARGARET I like the new tire within excellently, if the
hair were a thought browner; and your gown's a
most rare fashion, i'faith. I saw the Duchess of
Milan's gown that they praise so.

HERO O that exceeds, they say.

MARGARET By my troth, 's but a night-gown in respect
of yours – cloth o' gold and cuts, and laced with
silver, set with pearls, down-sleeves, side-sleeves, 20
and skirts, round underborne with a bluish tinsel;
but for a fine, quaint, graceful and excellent
fashion, yours is worth ten on't.

HERO God give me joy to wear it, for my heart is
exceeding heavy.

MARGARET 'Twill be heavier soon, by the weight of a
man.

HERO Fie upon thee; art not ashamed?

MARGARET Of what, lady? Of speaking honourably?
Is not marriage honourable in a beggar? Is not 30
your lord honourable without marriage? I think
you would have me say 'saving your reverence, a
husband'; an bad thinking do not wrest true
speaking, I'll offend nobody. Is there any harm in
'the heavier for a husband'? None, I think, an it be
the right husband and the right wife; otherwise 'tis
light and not heavy. Ask my Lady Beatrice else –
here she comes.

Enter BEATRICE

HERO Good morrow, coz.

BEATRICE Good morrow, sweet Hero. 40

[41] tune *mood*

[42] out of all other tune *Beatrice continues the metaphor.*

[43] Clap's *clap us (i.e. clap the beat)*

Light O'love *A popular dance tune.*

[43–4] that goes without a burden *that can be sung without a bass line; which, for Margaret, means without being 'heavier for a husband'.*

[45] Ye . . . heels *(1) you go dance it (2) you're wanton yourself*

[46] have stables enough *(1) is rich enough (2) provides enough opportunities*

[46–7] you'll . . . barns *you'll make sure he doesn't lack children;* barns: *bairns*

[48] O illegitimate construction *i.e. what a wicked suggestion (punning on* illegitimate *in connection with* barns)

[52] Heigh-ho *Reminiscent of her reference to the ballad (at II.1.314); a means of summoning someone or something.*

[54] For the letter . . . H *Ache was pronounced like H.*

[56] an you be not turned Turk *i.e. if you haven't changed your faith (by falling in love)*

[56–7] there's . . . star *it's no longer safe to use the Pole star as a guide (i.e. nothing's certain any more)*

[58] trow *I wonder (Beatrice affects not to know what Margaret is talking about)*

[62] I am stuffed *i.e. with a head cold (the reason why Beatrice did not share Hero's bed, see IV.1.147)*

[63] A maid, and stuffed *Margaret picks up the word in mock-horror at its other interpretation, that Beatrice is not a virgin.*

[63–4] There's goodly *that's a fine result (from catching a cold)*

[66] professed apprehension *claimed to have a quick wit*

[67] left it *abandoned it (because of the other things on your mind)*

[68] become me rarely *suit me very well (i.e. aren't I good at it?)*

[69–70] It . . . cap *Beatrice is being ironical, suggesting Margaret should display her wit even more. Also a pun on* become, *as though she is wearing her wit.*

[71–2] this distilled Carduus Benedictus *Margaret prescribes for Beatrice a medicine made from a herb (the blessed thistle). It was thought to cure many afflictions, including heart disease.*

[72] lay it to your heart *i.e. to cure it (with the suggestion of holding the actual Benedick closely)*

[73] qualm *sudden sickness*

HERO Why, how now? Do you speak in the sick tune?

BEATRICE I am out of all other tune, methinks.

MARGARET Clap's into 'Light o' love' – that goes without a burden. Do you sing it and I'll dance it.

BEATRICE Ye light o' love with your heels! Then if your husband have stables enough, you'll see he shall lack no barns.

MARGARET O illegitimate construction! I scorn that with my heels.

BEATRICE 'Tis almost five o'clock, cousin; 'tis time 50
you were ready. By my troth, I am exceeding ill. Heigh-ho!

MARGARET For a hawk, a horse, or a husband?

BEATRICE For the letter that begins them all, H.

MARGARET Well, an you be not turned Turk, there's no more sailing by the star.

BEATRICE What means the fool, trow?

MARGARET Nothing I; but God send everyone their heart's desire!

HERO These gloves the Count sent me; they are an 60
excellent perfume.

BEATRICE I am stuffed, cousin; I cannot smell.

MARGARET A maid and stuffed! There's goodly catching of cold.

BEATRICE O, God help me, God help me! How long have you professed apprehension?

MARGARET Ever since you left it. Doth not my wit become me rarely?

BEATRICE It is not seen enough; you should wear it in your cap. By my troth, I am sick. 70

MARGARET Get you some of this distilled Carduus Benedictus and lay it to your heart; it is the only thing for a qualm.

[74] There . . . thistle   *i.e. you've touched a sore point (the need to have the medicine, i.e. Benedick, as a cure). Hero makes the bawdiest joke in the scene.*

[77–8] I have no moral meaning   *She puns with delight on* moral *as (1) hidden meaning (2) correct intention.*

[79] perchance   *perhaps*
[80] by'r lady   *by our Lady*
[81] list   *please*
[82] if I would   *even if I could*
[85] such another   *just like that*
become a man   *The implication is that Benedick was not 'complete' until he loved.*

[87–8] he eats his meat without grudging   *i.e. he's content to be in love (see back to II.1.148)*

[88] may be   *might be, or could have been*

[89] look with your eyes   *The eye was considered the agent of passion; Margaret is saying that Beatrice is perfectly aware of men.*

[92] Not a false gallop   *i.e. not an artificial step (and hence, true)*
[93] withdraw   *retire (in order to dress)*
[94] gallants   *young men*

ACT THREE, scene 5

Dogberry, determined not to be denied his moment of glory, generates acute suspense through his self-important report of the arrest.

[1] would you   *do you want*
[3] confidence   *(for* conference*)*
[4] decerns *(for* concerns*)*
nearly   *closely*

HERO There thou prickest her with a thistle.

BEATRICE Benedictus? Why Benedictus? You have some moral in this Benedictus?

MARGARET Moral? No, by my troth, I have no moral meaning; I meant plain holy-thistle. You may think perchance that I think you are in love? Nay, by'r lady, I am not such a fool to think what I list, 80 nor I list not to think what I can; nor indeed I cannot think, if I would think my heart out of thinking, that you are in love, or that you will be in love, or that you can be in love. Yet Benedick was such another, and now is he become a man; he swore he would never marry, and yet now, in despite of his heart, he eats his meat without grudging. And how you may be converted, I know not; but methinks you look with your eyes as other women do. 90

BEATRICE What pace is this that thy tongue keeps?

MARGARET Not a false gallop.

Enter URSULA

URSULA Madam, withdraw. The Prince, the Count, Signor Benedick, Don John and all the gallants of the town are come to fetch you to church.

HERO Help to dress me, good coz, good Meg, good Ursula.

[*Exeunt*

Scene 5. *Enter* LEONATO, DOGBERRY *and* VERGES

LEONATO What would you with me, honest neighbour?

DOGBERRY Marry, sir, I would have some confidence with you, that decerns you nearly.

[10–11] a little off the matter   *a little irrelevantly*

[12] blunt   *(for sharp)*

[13] as the skin . . . brows   *The forehead was held to be an indicator of character.*

[14–15] I am . . . than I   *I am as honest as any other old man who is no more honest than I am (thus he makes his claim absurd)*

[16] odorous   *(for odious)*

palabras   *(for pocas palabras, Spanish for 'few words'; a phrase in common use at the time)*

[18] tedious   *long-winded*

[21] if . . . king   *Dogberry thinks tedious means rich and is therefore a compliment. Through the mistake Shakespeare can slip in another joke against authority.*

[22] bestow it all of   *give it all to*

[24] and 'twere   *even if it were*

[25] exclamation on   *complaint of (for acclamation of)*

[29] fain ·   *gladly (Leonato's patience is wearing thin)*

[31] ha' ta'en   *have arrested*

[34] When the age is in   *He misquotes a saying, 'When the ale is in'. In fact, Verges is more direct than Dogberry.*

[36] God's a good man   *Another proverb, meaning 'God is good'.*

[36–7] an . . . behind   *Dogberry implies that God is fair, because one person (himself) is always superior to another (Verges).*

LEONATO Brief, I pray you, for you see it is a busy time
with me.

DOGBERRY Marry, this it is, sir,

VERGES Yes, in truth it is, sir.

LEONATO What is it, my good friends?

DOGBERRY Goodman Verges, sir, speaks a little off the 10
matter – an old man, sir, and his wits are not so
blunt as, God help, I would desire they were; but,
in faith, honest, as the skin between his brows.

VERGES Yes, I thank God, I am as honest as any man
living that is an old man and no honester than I.

DOGBERRY Comparisons are odorous; *palabras*, neighbour Verges.

LEONATO Neighbours, you are tedious.

DOGBERRY It pleases your worship to say so, but we
are the poor Duke's officers. But truly for mine own 20
part, if I were as tedious as a king, I could find in my
heart to bestow it all of your worship.

LEONATO All thy tediousness on me, ah?

DOGBERRY Yea, and 'twere a thousand pound more
than 'tis, for I hear as good exclamation on your
worship as of any man in the city, and though I be
but a poor man, I am glad to hear it.

VERGES And so am I.

LEONATO I would fain know what you have to say.

VERGES Marry, sir, our watch tonight, excepting your 30
worship's presence, ha' ta'en a couple of as arrant
knaves as any in Messina.

DOGBERRY A good old man, sir, he will be talking; as
they say, 'When the age is in, the wit is out'. God
help us, it is a world to see! Well said i'faith,
neighbour Verges; well, God's a good man, an two
men ride of a horse, one must ride behind. An

[38] An honest soul   *His favourite attribute again.*

[41–2] too short of you   *falls short of you (meaning he isn't as large)*

[43] Gifts that God gives   *Dogberry tries to be modest, thinking Leonato is flattering him.*

[46] comprehended   *(for apprehended)*

aspicious   *auspicious (for suspicious)*

[52] suffigance   *(for sufficient)*

[54] stay   *are waiting*

[56] wait upon   *accompany*

[57–8] Francis Seacoal   *The Sexton (and parish clerk) who appears in IV.2.*

[58] inkhorn   *horn in which ink was kept, often slung from the waist*

[59] examination   *(for examine)*

[61] We will spare for no wit   *Spare is ambiguous; he means they will give it the utmost attention; but it could also mean that they won't waste any intelligence on it – another joke at their expense.*

[62] non-come   *short for non compos mentis i.e. insane*

[64] excommunication   *(for examination)*

honest soul i'faith, sir, by my troth he is, as ever
broke bread. But – God is to be worshipped – all
men are not alike; alas, good neighbour!   40

LEONATO Indeed, neighbour, he comes too short of
you.

DOGBERRY Gifts that God gives.

LEONATO I must leave you.

DOGBERRY One word, sir. Our watch, sir, have indeed
comprehended two aspicious persons, and we
would have them this morning examined before
your worship.

LEONATO Take their examination yourself, and bring
it me. I am now in great haste, as it may appear   50
unto you.

DOGBERRY It shall be suffigance.

LEONATO Drink some wine ere you go; fare you well.

Enter a MESSENGER

MESSENGER My lord, they stay for you, to give your
daughter to her husband.

LEONATO I'll wait upon them; I am ready.

[*Exeunt* LEONATO *and* MESSENGER

DOGBERRY Go, good partner, go get you to Francis
Seacoal; bid him bring his pen and inkhorn to the
gaol. We are now to examination these men.

VERGES And we must do it wisely.   60

DOGBERRY We will spare for no wit, I warrant you.
Here's that shall drive some of them to a non-come;
only get the learned writer, to set down our
excommunication, and meet me at the gaol.

[*Exeunt*

ACT FOUR, scene 1

The first part of this scene, set in the church full of wedding guests, is powerful, and our knowledge of the truth intensifies rather than diminishes the dramatic impact. However, the emergence of a new 'practioner' whose motives are neither sport nor malice, brings hope; and there is another upward move at the end, in that Hero's misfortunes promote the consolidation of the other match. These two facts provide a dramatic balance to the disaster, and there is a fine modulation in the scene from viciousness, through the consolation of the Friar's confidence, to love in two guises – fierce loyalty and honest recognition.

[1] be brief – only to   *His haste echoes his impatience in the previous scene, when he has been too rushed to hear Dogberry's news.*

[2–3] recount . . . afterwards   *go over the rest of it after. The full service began with a lengthy discourse on the principles and responsibilities of Christian marriage.*

[6] To be married to her   *Leonato assumes that Claudio is quibbling.*

[11] inward   *hidden*

[13] on your souls   *on fear of losing salvation*

[14] Know you any   *Claudio repeats the question to Hero with ominous care.*

[17] I dare . . . answer   *Leonato is still full of cheerful confidence.*

[18–19] O, what . . . do   *These scathing exclamations begin to reveal Claudio's fury at being deceived. They fall like a blight on the atmosphere of the scene.*

[20] interjections   *expressions of feeling (a grammatical term – e.g. Claudio's O)*

[21] ah, ha, he   *Alternative forms of interjection, provided by Benedick in an attempt to counteract the sudden disturbance caused by Claudio's tone.*

[22] Stand thee by   *Step aside (the Friar complies silently, with productive result – see l. 154 ff.)*

by your leave   *i.e. if I may call you that*

[24] this maid, your daughter   *His deliberate emphasis prepares for the dramatic climax.*

[25] As freely . . . me   *Leonato is momentarily fooled by Claudio's apparent friendship.*

ACT FOUR

Scene 1. *Enter* DON PEDRO, DON JOHN, LEONATO, FRIAR, CLAUDIO, BENEDICK, HERO, BEATRICE *and* ATTENDANTS

LEONATO Come Friar Francis, be brief – only to the plain form of marriage, and you shall recount their particular duties afterwards.

FRIAR You come hither, my lord, to marry this lady?

CLAUDIO No.

LEONATO To be married to her, Friar; you come to marry her!

FRIAR Lady, you come hither to be married to this Count?

HERO I do.   10

FRIAR If either of you know any inward impediment why you should not be conjoined, I charge you on your souls to utter it.

CLAUDIO Know you any, Hero?

HERO None, my lord.

FRIAR Know you any, Count?

LEONATO I dare make his answer – none.

CLAUDIO O, what men dare do! What men may do! What men daily do, not knowing what they do!

BENEDICK How now – interjections? Why then, some   20
be of laughing, as ah, ha, he!

CLAUDIO Stand thee by, Friar. Father, by your
          leave,
    Will you with free and unconstrainèd soul
    Give me this maid, your daughter?

LEONATO As freely, son, as God did give her me.

[27] counterpoise   *balance (i.e. repay)*

[28] render her again   *give her back again*

[29] learn   *teach. The audience has a sense of their unpleasant collusion in this exchange; Claudio is exaggeratedly grateful to Don Pedro, then abrupt with Leonato.*

[31] this rotten orange   *A powerful image for something that only appears to be wholesome. Oranges were luxury items, and rotten was often used in alluding to venereal disease (the* rot*); thus he implies she is a whore.*

[32] but the sign and semblance   *only the outward appearance and imitation*

[33] Behold . . . here   *He begins now his cruel assertions of her guilt, addressing the congregation at large.*

[34–5] O, what . . . withal   *The terrible irony of these statements is that they are of course true; but he is applying them to the wrong person.*

[36] that blood as modest evidence   *her blush as proof of her modesty. Both of his questions seek to convince his audience that the evidence of their eyes (her appearance) may not be believed. Yet how else has he come to believe what Don John has told him? (See III.2.114.)*

[39] shows   *appearances*
But she is none   *The denial has considerable force after Claudio has softened his listeners so skilfully.*

[40] She knows . . . bed   *she's familiar with the pleasures of sex;* luxurious*: lustful*

[42] Not to be married   *He twists Leonato's question and takes* mean *as intend.*

[43] an approvèd wanton   *(1) someone known to be a 'loose woman' (2) an experienced whore. (He uses* soul *deliberately, to contrast her with the purity of his own intentions.)*

[44] in your own proof   *in testing her virtue yourself*

[47] what you would say   *what you are suggesting*
known her   *i.e. sexually*

[48] as a husband   *as if I were already her husband*

[49] extenuate the 'forehand sin   *excuse the fact that we've anticipated the wedding. Engagements were considered legally binding at that time.* 'forehand: *beforehand*

[51] large   *suggestive*

[53] comely love   *i.e. he's been suitably controlled*

He places her hand in CLAUDIO's

CLAUDIO And what have I to give you back, whose worth

May counterpoise this rich and precious gift?

DON PEDRO Nothing, unless you render her again.

CLAUDIO Sweet Prince, you learn me noble thankfulness.

There, Leonato, take her back again.   30

Give not this rotten orange to your friend;

She's but the sign and semblance of her honour.

Behold, how like a maid she blushes here!

O, what authority and show of truth

Can cunning sin cover itself withal!

Comes not that blood as modest evidence

To witness simple virtue? Would you not swear,

All you that see her, that she were a maid

By these exterior shows? But she is none.

She knows the heat of a luxurious bed;   40

Her blush is guiltiness, not modesty.

LEONATO What do you mean, my lord?

CLAUDIO   Not to be married,

Not to knit my soul to an approvèd wanton.

LEONATO Dear my lord, if you in your own proof

Have vanquished the resistance of her youth,

And made defeat of her virginity –

CLAUDIO I know what you would say. If I have known her,

You will say she did embrace me as a husband,

And so extenuate the 'forehand sin.

No, Leonato,   50

I never tempted her with word too large,

But, as a brother to his sister, showed

Bashful sincerity and comely love.

[54] And seemed . . . you   *She appears to stress the verb deliberately – is she bewildered, or angrily incredulous?*

[55] Out on thee seeming   *i.e. to hell with your seeming*
write against it   *denounce you formally. His denunciation is measured like a curse as he contrasts what she seems and what (to him) she is.*

[56–7] as Dian . . . be blown   *Both similes are archetypes of purity. (Diana, the virgin goddess of the Moon, is in direct contrast to Venus, goddess of Love, at l. 59.)*

[56] her orb   *i.e. the moon*

[57] blown   *in full blossom*

[58] more intemperate in your blood   *of more undisciplined sensuality (promiscuous)*

[59] pampered   *i.e. because they can gratify their instincts without constraints*

[60] That . . . sensuality   *that burn with wild sensual pleasure*

[61] so wide   *so mistakenly (literally: wide of the mark, off-target) Her single line is clipped and powerful in contrast to his wordy attack.*

[62] What should I speak   *what is there to say*

[63] that   *i.e. I who*

[64] stale   *prostitute*

[65] do I but dream   *Leonato hopes even yet that the present reality is only a 'seeming truth'.*

[67] nuptial   *wedding*

[70] Are our eyes our own   *can't we believe our own eyes; a heavy irony, since the audience knows that Claudio sees with the 'borrowed eyes' of Don John's malice.*

[72] move   *put*

[73] that fatherly and kindly power   *by your natural authority as her father*

[76] beset   *attacked from all sides*

[77] catechising   *questioning. The catechism is the set of questions on the Christian faith to be learnt before confirmation; their questions must be answered before she can be 'confirmed' as ready for marriage. It was also the practice to catechise women suspected of being witches.*

[77] to your name   *on oath. Also, the first question of the catechism asks, 'What is your name?'*

HERO And seemed I ever otherwise to you?

CLAUDIO Out on thee seeming! I will write against
    it:
    You seem to me as Dian in her orb,
    As chaste as is the bud ere it be blown.
    But you are more intemperate in your blood
    Than Venus, or those pampered animals
    That rage in savage sensuality.   60

HERO Is my lord well, that he doth speak so wide?

LEONATO Sweet Prince, why speak not you?

DON PEDRO   What should I speak?
    I stand dishonoured, that have gone about
    To link my dear friend to a common stale.

LEONATO Are these things spoken, or do I but
    dream?

DON JOHN Sir, they are spoken, and these things are
    true.

BENEDICK [*Aside*] This looks not like a nuptial.

HERO   True? O God!

CLAUDIO Leonato, stand I here?
    Is this the Prince? Is this the Prince's brother?
    Is this face Hero's? Are our eyes our own?   70

LEONATO All this is so, but what of this, my lord?

CLAUDIO Let me but move one question to your
    daughter,
    And by that fatherly and kindly power
    That you have in her, bid her answer truly.

LEONATO I charge thee do so, as thou art my child.

HERO O God defend me, how am I beset!
    What kind of catechising call you this?

CLAUDIO To make you answer truly to your name.

HERO Is it not Hero? Who can blot that name
    With any just reproach?

[80] that can Hero   *i.e. the name itself can do that*

[84] Now . . . this   *His injunction is uttered with the triumphant confidence of a closed mind: any answer she gives will be wrong.*

answer to this   *explain that (if you can)*

[85] I talked . . . hour   *Ironically her denial 'proves' her guilt, since their minds are already made up.*

[86] no maiden   *He echoes no man.*

[88] grievèd   *wronged (rather than saddened; his honour is at stake)*

[91] who hath indeed   *This indicates another detail of the deception which has taken place off-stage (mentioned by Borachio at III.3.146).*

liberal   *dissolute (also suggesting he has been liberal with details)*

[94] Fie, fie   *Don John continues his show of moral horror.*

[96–7] There . . . them   *i.e. even the words used to describe her activities couldn't be uttered without giving offence. An easy way of implying the worst, without having to give details (as at III.2.105).*

[97] Thus   *suffice it to say (pretty lady stresses how she appears)*

[98] thy much misgovernment   *your appalling behaviour. This direct reproof of her achieves new depths in Don John's hypocrisy.*

[99–107] O Hero . . . be gracious   *Claudio's speech now laments her in a more conventional way, softened by the way he evokes her attractions, and making the traditional resolutions of the deceived lover.*

[99] what a Hero hadst thou been   *(1) how marvellous you would have been (2) possibly a reference to the devotion of Hero in the Greek legend of Hero and Leander (who commits suicide rather than live without her lover)*

[100–1] If half . . . heart   *i.e. if half the beauty of your appearance had gone to make you pure in mind and feeling also*

[102] most foul, most fair   *He is again formalising his double response to her.*

[103] pure impiety and impious purity   *The same contradictions – she is his oxymoron; impiety: wickedness*

[104] For thee   *i.e. on account of what you have done to me*

[104–6] I'll lock . . . harm   *i.e. he's not going to love again. The elaborate image, of closing the gates and hanging suspicion like padlocks on his eyelids, again identifies the eye as the agent of love. The eyes, guarded by suspicion, will henceforth see beauty as dangerous.*

[107] more   *again*

gracious   *attractive (to me)*

CLAUDIO   Marry, that can Hero: 80
    Hero itself can blot out Hero's virtue.
    What man was he talked with you yesternight,
    Out at your window betwixt twelve and one?
    Now, if you are a maid, answer to this.

HERO I talked with no man at that hour, my lord.

DON PEDRO Why, then are you no maiden. Leonato,
    I am sorry you must hear. Upon mine honour,
    Myself, my brother, and this grievèd Count
    Did see her, hear her, at that hour last night
    Talk with a ruffian at her chamber window;   90
    Who hath indeed, most like a liberal villain,
    Confessed the vile encounters they have had
    A thousand times in secret.

DON JOHN Fie, fie, they are not to be named, my
      lord,
    Not to be spoke of!
    There is not chastity enough in language
    Without offence to utter them. Thus, pretty
      lady,
    I am sorry for thy much misgovernment.

CLAUDIO O Hero, what a Hero hadst thou been,
    If half thy outward graces had been placed   100
    About thy thoughts and counsels of thy heart!
    But fare thee well, most foul, most fair; farewell
    Thou pure impiety, and impious purity!
    For thee I'll lock up all the gates of love
    And on my eyelids shall conjecture hang,
    To turn all beauty into thoughts of harm,
    And never shall it more be gracious.

LEONATO Hath no man's dagger here a point for
      me?

[HERO collapses] *The point at which she collapses is important; it is not the accusations, but her own father's belief in them which astounds her (see Introduction, p. 16).*

[110] these things *i.e. the alleged 'vile encounters'*

[111] Smother . . . up *overcome her will to live*

[Exeunt . . . CLAUDIO] *It is important to the plot that they leave before Hero has recovered; and important to Don John to remove the others before any doubts might arise.*

[114] take not away thy heavy hand *i.e. if she seems dead, let her stay so (since that is the only honourable solution)*

[115] fairest *most suitable*

[118] Dost thou look up *His tone is reproachful, in contrast to the concern of Beatrice and the Friar.*

[119–42] Wherefore . . . flesh *Leonato now details his rejection of Hero. The force of his anger has to be seen in the context of his society, where a high value is set on 'honour'; and where suggestive word-play is a pastime for wit, but not a guideline for morals (see Introduction, p. 13).*

[121] printed in her blood *(1) shown by her blush (2) indelibly marked on her life*

[123] For did I think *if I thought*

[124] Thought I *if I thought*

spirits *physical being (since in fainting he assumes her shames have overcome her, as Don John has suggested)*

[125] on the rearward of reproaches *as sequel to the way I've reproached you*

[126] Grieved I, I had but one *can I really have lamented the fact that I had only one child*

[127] Chid . . . frame *can I really have cursed nature for being so mean*

[128] why had I one *why did I even have one*

HERO *collapses*

BEATRICE Why how now, cousin, wherefore sink
    you down?
DON JOHN Come, let us go; these things, come thus
    to light,   110
    Smother her spirits up.
        [*Exeunt* DON PEDRO, DON JOHN *and* CLAUDIO
BENEDICK How doth the lady?
BEATRICE   Dead, I think – help, uncle!
    Hero? Why, Hero! Uncle! Signor Benedick! Friar!
LEONATO O Fate, take not away thy heavy hand!
    Death is the fairest cover for her shame
    That may be wished for.
BEATRICE   How now, cousin Hero?

HERO *begins to revive*

FRIAR Have comfort, lady.
LEONATO Dost thou look up?
FRIAR   Yea, wherefore should she not?
LEONATO Wherefore? Why, doth not every earthly
    thing
    Cry shame upon her? Could she here deny   120
    The story that is printed in her blood?
    Do not live, Hero, do not ope thine eyes.
    For did I think thou wouldst not quickly die,
    Thought I thy spirits were strong than thy
    shames,
    Myself would – on the rearward of reproaches –
    Strike at thy life. Grieved I, I had but one?
    Chid I for that at frugal Nature's frame?
    O, one too much by thee; why had I one?
    Why ever wast thou lovely in my eyes?

[130] with charitable hand   *as an act of charity*

[131] issue   *child*

[132] who smirchèd thus and mired with infamy   *who sullied and disgraced by such wickedness as she is now*

[135–8] But mine . . . of her   *The repetition of* mine *can be seen as exhibiting his real anguish; but what motivates it – the dishonour she has brought on herself, or the dishonour she has brought him?*

[137–8] That I . . . of her   *my estimation of her was so high that my own interests gave way to her*

[138–9] she is fallen/Into a pit of ink   *The crescendo built, the actual peak is achieved with a metaphor that picks up Hero's* 'Who can blot that name' *(l. 79). For Leonato, the ink stains her reputation beyond redemption.*

[141–2] And salt . . . flesh   *i.e. there isn't enough salt in the sea to make her wholesome. The Elizabethans would be used to bad meat which needed salt to disguise the flavour; and* tainted flesh *could be the metaphorical result of the 'sins of the flesh'.*

[143] attired in wonder   *so totally bemused*

[145] belied   *slandered; a rapid and positive refusal to accept the 'evidence', ardently contradicting Leonato's detailed lament.*

[149] that   *i.e. the evidence against her (is stronger than ever – as it would be, to the mind that is already convinced)*

[152] that speaking   *that while speaking*

[153] Hence from her   *get away from her*

[156] given way unto   *allowed things to proceed to*

[157] By noting of the lady   *in order to observe her. At last a voice of calm reason is heard; the verb recalls Claudio's first discussion of his love (at I.1.158).*

Why had I not with charitable hand 130
Took up a beggar's issue at my gates,
Who smirchèd thus and mired with infamy,
I might have said, 'No part of it is mine;
This shame derives itself from unknown loins'?
But mine, and mine I loved, and mine I
   praised,
And mine that I was proud on, mine so much
That I myself was to myself not mine,
Valuing of her – why she, O she is fall'n
Into a pit of ink, that the wide sea
Hath drops too few to wash her clean again, 140
And salt too little which may season give
To her foul tainted flesh!

BENEDICK   Sir, sir, be patient.
   For my part, I am so attired in wonder,
   I know not what to say.

BEATRICE O, on my soul, my cousin is belied!

BENEDICK Lady, were you her bedfellow last
      night?

BEATRICE No, truly, not, although until last night
   I have this twelvemonth been her bedfellow.

LEONATO Confirmed, confirmed! O, that is stronger
      made,
   Which was before barred up with ribs of iron! 150
   Would the two Princes lie? And Claudio lie –
   Who loved her so, that speaking of her foulness,
   Washed it with tears? Hence from her – let her
      die!

FRIAR Hear me a little;
   For I have only silent been so long,
   And given way unto this course of fortune,
   By noting of the lady. I have marked

[158] blushing apparitions *appearances of blushing*

[159] innocent shames *signs of innocent modesty*

[161–2] a fire/To burn the errors *i.e. as though Don Pedro and Don John are heretics (for not believing in her)*

[163–9] Call me . . . biting error *The Friar now stakes his whole professional and spiritual reputation on Hero being innocent. His confidence in his observations nicely balances Leonato's too-ready acceptance of secondhand evidence, and from this point the Friar takes control.*

[164] reading *i.e. theoretical learning*

[165–6] Which . . . book *which, confirmed by experience, can guarantee what I have learnt*

[167] My reverence, calling, nor divinity *the respect due to me as a priest, my vocation, nor my theological expertise*

[169] some biting error *His adjective conveys an understanding of how Hero must be feeling, and recalls Don John at I.3.33.*

[172] perjury *lying under oath*

not denies *does not deny (she hasn't been asked since her first denial was taken as proof of guilt)*

[173] cover *(as with clothes)*

[174] proper nakedness *appropriately stark*

[175] of *i.e. of being with*

[176] I know none *(1) I don't know who it could be (2) I don't know any man in that way (i.e. intimately)*

[178] warrant *permit*

[179] Let . . . mercy *A strong invocation which would have particular force with the Friar.*

[179–83] O my father . . . to death *The rest of her speech could be addressed to the Friar as priest, or to Leonato; my suggests the latter, but the appeal answers the Friar's question and is in response to his confidence in her.*

[181] unmeet *improper*   [182] change *exchange*

[183] Refuse me, hate me, torture me *Addressed to the Friar, refuse would mean 'deny me absolution' (compare l. 179) whereas hate has more relevance for Leonato. She seems to be asking for total rejection – spiritual, emotional and physical – and could be appealing to them both simultaneously.*

[184] There . . . Princes *The force of Hero's speech confirms the Friar's judgement.* misprision: *misunderstanding (compare III.1.52)*

[185] the very bent of honour *the essence of honour; an archery metaphor from the bow fully poised (compare II.3.224)*

A thousand blushing apparitions
To start into her face, a thousand innocent
    shames
In angel whiteness beat away those blushes;   160
And in her eye there hath appeared a fire,
To burn the errors that these Princes hold
Against her maiden truth. Call me a fool;
Trust not my reading, nor my observations,
Which with experimental seal doth warrant
The tenor of my book; trust not my age,
My reverence, calling, nor divinity,
If this sweet lady lie not guiltless here,
Under some biting error.

LEONATO   Friar, it cannot be.
Thou seest that all the grace that she hath left   170
Is that she will not add to her damnation
A sin of perjury; she not denies it.
Why seek'st thou then to cover with excuse
That which appears in proper nakedness?

FRIAR Lady, what man is he you are accused of?

HERO They know that do accuse me; I know none.
If I know more of any man alive
Than that which maiden modesty doth
    warrant,
Let all my sins lack mercy! O my father,
Prove you that any man with me conversed   180
At hours unmeet, or that I yesternight
Maintained the change of words with any
    creature,
Refuse me, hate me, torture me to death!

FRIAR There is some strange misprision in the
    Princes.

BENEDICK Two of them have the very bent of

[187] The practice . . . Bastard   *i.e. Don John is the one who has contrived it. Compare II.2.51-2*, Grow this to what adverse issue it can, I will put it in practice.

[188] whose . . . villainies   *whose whole being labours to make trouble. If Benedick knows this, why do Don Pedro and Claudio not suspect him also?*

[189] I know not   *i.e. I don't know what to think*

[190] These hands shall tear her   *A reaction which becomes much more violent on stage where it is confronted with Hero's evident attractiveness.*

[191] proudest   *highest in rank*

[192] Time . . . mine   *i.e. I'm not that old*

[193] invention   *scheming imagination*

[194] means   *wealth*

[195] Nor my bad life reft   *nor has my life been so bad as to deprive*

[196] in such a kind   *for a cause like this*

[197] policy of mind   *inventiveness*

[199] to quit me of them   *to get even with them (for such an insult)* throughly   *thoroughly*

[200] let my counsel sway you   *be influenced by my advice. The Friar now plans another kind of* practice.

[202] kept in   *i.e. hidden*

[203] publish   *make it known*

[204] a mourning ostentation   *a display of formal mourning*

[205] monument   *family vault (in which many generations of the same family were buried)*

[207] appertain unto   *are appropriate for*

[208] become of   *result from*

[209] well carried   *effectively sustained*

[210] remorse   *pity*

[211] that   *i.e. that result*

[212] But on . . . birth   *but from this labour (work/childbirth) expect a better outcome*

    honour
    And if their wisdoms be misled in this,
    The practice of it lives in John the Bastard
    Whose spirits toil in frame of villainies.
LEONATO I know not. If they speak but truth of her,
    These hands shall tear her; if they wrong her
      honour,   190
    The proudest of them shall well hear of it.
    Time hath not yet so dried this blood of mine,
    Nor age so eat up my invention,
    Nor fortune made such havoc of my means,
    Nor my bad life reft me so much of friends,
    But they shall find, awaked in such a kind,
    Both strength of limb and policy of mind,
    Ability in means and choice of friends,
    To quit me of them throughly.
FRIAR   Pause awhile,
    And let my counsel sway you in this case.   200
    Your daughter here the Princes left for dead;
    Let her awhile be secretly kept in,
    And publish it that she is dead indeed.
    Maintain a mourning ostentation,
    And on your family's old monument
    Hang mournful epitaphs and do all rites
    That appertain unto a burial.
LEONATO What shall become of this? What will this
    do?
FRIAR Marry, this, well carried, shall on her behalf
    Change slander to remorse; that is some good.   210
    But not for that dream I on this strange course,
    But on this travail look for greater birth.
    She dying, as it must be so maintained,
    Upon the instant that she was accused,

[216–21] For it so . . . was ours   *The Friar now goes on to explain the psychology of his plan.*

[217] to the worth   *for its real value*

[219] rack the value   *over-estimate the value;* rack: *the torture instrument on which a person was stretched*

[223] Th' idea of her life   *the image of how she was*

[224] study of imagination   *quiet moments of reflection*

[225] organ of her life   *(each) part of her living being*

[226] apparelled in more precious habit   *i.e. appear more beautifully dressed*

[227] moving-delicate   *touching in its fineness*

[228] Into the eye and prospect of his soul   *within range of the vision of his innermost being*

[229] Than when she lived indeed   *than when she was actually alive*

[230] in his liver   *Like the heart, the liver was considered a source of the passions.*

[233] success   *what will follow*

[234–5] fashion . . . likelihood   *the actual result will be better than my account of what is possible;* event: *outcome*

[236] But if . . . false   *even if this is the only result;* aim *and* levelled *are both archery terms*

[237–8] The supposition . . . infamy   *the news of her supposed death will abate the amazement roused by her notoriety*

[239] sort   *turn out*

[241] reclusive   *hidden (as a nun)*

[242] eyes, tongues, minds and injuries   *He maps the typical process of slander – from what is seen, to what is talked about, to the mind's interpretation, to the actual harm.*

[244] inwardness   *loyalty as a friend*

[246] deal in this   *treat this matter*

Shall be lamented, pitied and excused
Of every hearer. For it so falls out
That what we have we prize not to the worth,
Whiles we enjoy it; but being lacked and lost
Why then we rack the value, then we find
The virtue that possession would not show us   220
Whiles it was ours. So will it fare with Claudio.
When he shall hear she died upon his words,
Th' idea of her life shall sweetly creep
Into his study of imagination;
And every lovely organ of her life
Shall come apparelled in more precious habit,
More moving-delicate and full of life,
Into the eye and prospect of his soul
Than when she lived indeed. Then shall he
   mourn,
If ever love had interest in his liver,   230
And wish he had not so accusèd her;
No, though he thought his accusation true.
Let this be so, and doubt not but success
Will fashion the event in better shape
Than I can lay it down in likelihood.
But if all aim but this be levelled false,
The supposition of the lady's death
Will quench the wonder of her infamy.
And if it sort not well, you may conceal her –
As best befits her wounded reputation –   240
In some reclusive and religious life,
Out of all eyes, tongues, minds and injuries.
BENEDICK Signor Leonato, let the Friar advise you;
And though you know my inwardness and love
Is very much unto the Prince and Claudio,
Yet, by mine honour, I will deal in this

[247–8] As . . . body *with the same discretion and integrity as you would with your own inmost thoughts*

[248] Being that *since*

[249] The smallest . . . me *Leonato's image suggests that in his distress he is 'afloat' from not knowing what to think, and may be easily led by any suggestion.* twine: *thread*

[250] Presently away *let's go at once*

[251] For . . . cure *Compare the maxim 'Desperate diseases demand desperate remedies' – an early medical theory.*

strangely *ingeniously*

strain *make great effort with*

[253] prolonged *postponed*

[Exeunt . . . BENEDICK] *The crisis in one match provides an opportunity for consolidation in the other. It is the first time Beatrice and Benedick have talked together on stage since Don Pedro's practice.*

[257] desire *want. Beatrice takes the meaning up as 'request'.*

[262] right her *(1) vindicate (2) antithesis of* wronged *in the previous line*

[264] even *straightforward*

no such friend *no one to fit the role of friend*

[266] but not yours *There seem to be two levels in this: (1) as a ghost of their previous sparring, implying that the task requires a man and Benedick doesn't qualify as such (2) Beatrice is acknowledging the nature of Benedick's relationship to Claudio, which would make it extremely difficult for him to issue a challenge.*

[269–73] As strange . . . cousin *This speech seems to demonstrate Beatrice's confusion at Benedick's sudden declaration; she is not quite ready to relinquish the mask of her former aggressiveness. A nice oscillation, which resorts to the topic of Hero as an escape route.*

[275] Do not swear and eat it *He swears on his sword; Beatrice says it would be better not to, in case he has to eat his word!*

As secretly and justly as your soul
Should with your body.

LEONATO   Being that I flow in grief
The smallest twine may lead me.

FRIAR 'Tis well consented. Presently away;   250
For to strange sores strangely they strain the
cure.
Come, lady, die to live – this wedding-day
Perhaps is but prolonged; have patience and
endure.

[*Exeunt all but* BEATRICE *and* BENEDICK

BENEDICK Lady Beatrice, have you wept all this
while?

BEATRICE Yea, and I will weep a while longer.

BENEDICK I will not desire that.

BEATRICE You have no reason; I do it freely.

BENEDICK Surely I do believe your fair cousin is
wronged.   260

BEATRICE Ah, how much might the man deserve of
me that would right her!

BENEDICK Is there any way to show such friendship?

BEATRICE A very even way, but no such friend.

BENEDICK May a man do it?

BEATRICE It is a man's office, but not yours.

BENEDICK I do love nothing in the world so well as
you; is not that strange?

BEATRICE As strange as the thing I know not; it were
as possible for me to say I loved nothing so well as   270
you. But believe me not; and yet I lie not. I confess
nothing, nor I deny nothing. I am sorry for my
cousin.

BENEDICK By my sword, Beatrice, thou lovest me.

BEATRICE Do not swear and eat it.

[279–80] With . . . to it *He won't (retract), whatever garnish might be made to go with his word.*
[280] protest *swear*
[283] stayed me in a happy hour *stopped me at a propitious moment (though why she asked God's forgiveness is not obvious; it could be for not taking him seriously here, or for past sharpness)*

[289] Kill Claudio *In contrast to the declarations of love, this is stark and sudden. Beatrice is quick to make use of a new weapon; instead of scorn, she can now use love to obtain what she wants.*
[291] deny it *refuse*

[293] I am gone though I am here *I'm physically here but my feelings are already elsewhere*
[296] will *intend to*

[301] Is 'a not . . . villain *is he not known to be a thorough villain (Beatrice's stored-up reactions now emerge)*
[303–4] bear her in hand *i.e. play her along (literally: escort her formally with her hand on his)* ·
[306] unmitigated rancour *undiluted bitterness*

BENEDICK I will swear by it that you love me, and I
   will make him eat it that says I love not you.

BEATRICE Will you not eat your word?

BENEDICK With no sauce that can be devised to it. I
   protest I love thee.   280

BEATRICE Why then, God forgive me!

BENEDICK What offence, sweet Beatrice?

BEATRICE You have stayed me in a happy hour; I was
   about to protest I loved you.

BENEDICK And do it with all thy heart.

BEATRICE I love you with so much of my heart that
   none is left to protest.

BENEDICK Come, bid me do anything for thee.

BEATRICE Kill Claudio.

BENEDICK Ha? Not for the wide world!   290

BEATRICE You kill me to deny it. Farewell.

BENEDICK Tarry, sweet Beatrice.

He takes her hand

BEATRICE I am gone, though I am here. There is no
   love in you. Nay, I pray you, let me go.

BENEDICK Beatrice?

BEATRICE In faith, I will go.

BENEDICK We'll be friends first.

BEATRICE You dare easier be friends with me than
   fight with mine enemy?

BENEDICK Is Claudio thine enemy?   300

BEATRICE Is 'a not approved in the height a villain
   that hath slandered, scorned, dishonoured my
   kinswoman? O that I were a man! What – bear her
   in hand until they come to take hands? And then
   with public accusation, uncovered slander, unmitigated rancour – O God, that I were a man! I

169

[307] in the market place   *i.e. in the most public place possible*

[310] A proper saying   *She speaks with heavy irony.*

[314] Beat —   *As Beatrice's indignation gathers momentum, Benedick's responses are curtailed!*

[315] counties   *counts*

[316] count   *A legal indictment (to match* testimony*), as well as a derisory reference to Claudio.*

Count Comfect   *Equivalent in derision to 'sugar-coated count' implying decorative uselessness and sickly sweetness, which is taken up in* sweet gallant. *It is also very similar to 'conte confect' — a made-up story.*

[317] for his sake   *i.e. so that I could fight him*

[319] curtsies   *courtly formalities. Her indictments are fierce; are they fair judgements on the court generally, or simply the result of her anger?*

[320] compliment   *flattery*

turned into tongue   *i.e. they are all talk (no action)*

[321] trim   *fine (she is being ironical)*

[321–2] He is . . . it   *to be called courageous these days you only have to make things happen in words*

[322–3] I cannot . . . wishing   *I can't change myself into a man simply by wanting to*

[332] engaged   *bound (to challenge Claudio)*

[333–4] By this hand   *an oath (as well as literally, the hand which holds the sword)*

[334] render me a dear account   *The metaphor makes Claudio in debt to Benedick now, as well as to Beatrice, which unifies them as the scene ends.* dear: *expensive; it will also be costly for Benedick, who is forsaking his friend.*

would eat his heart in the market-place.

BENEDICK Hear me, Beatrice –

BEATRICE Talk with a man, out at a window? A
proper saying!   310

BENEDICK Nay, but Beatrice –

BEATRICE Sweet Hero! She is wronged, she is slandered, she is undone.

BENEDICK Beat –

BEATRICE Princes and counties! Surely a princely
testimony, a goodly count, Count Comfect: a sweet
gallant, surely! O that I were a man for his sake; or
that I had any friend would be a man for my sake!
But manhood is melted into curtsies, valour into
compliment, and men are only turned into tongue – 320
and trim ones, too. He is now as valiant as Hercules
that only tells a lie and swears it. I cannot be a man
with wishing; therefore I will die a woman with
grieving.

BENEDICK Tarry, good Beatrice. By this hand, I love
thee.

BEATRICE Use it for my love some other way than
swearing by it.

BENEDICK Think you, in your soul, the Count Claudio
hath wronged Hero?   330

BEATRICE Yea, as sure as I have a thought or a soul.

BENEDICK Enough; I am engaged. I will challenge
him. I will kiss your hand, and so I leave you. By
this hand, Claudio shall render me a dear account.
As you hear of me, so think of me. Go comfort your
cousin; I must say she is dead; and so farewell.

[*Exeunt, separately*

ACT FOUR, scene 2

Slowly, slowly, the truth is released – here through the crucial and totally mis-conducted examination of the prisoners, and with the assistance of a new agent of justice. The scene takes place at the gaol (as mentioned at III. 5).

[1] dissembly *(for* assembly*)*

[4] that am I *Dogberry's consciousness of his position makes him seek the limelight.*

[5] exhibition *(for* commission*). Verges endorses and expands Dogberry's mistake.*

[10] let them come before me *He now takes on a judge-like role, immediately undermining it with the inappropriate informality of* friend.

[14] sirrah *A patronising form of address, to which Conrade reacts strongly.*

[17–18] Master Gentleman Conrade *In his ignorance Dogberry now over-elaborates the title.*

[19] we hope *The most likely meaning of this is that they hope for the life to come (i.e. a specifically religious use of* hope, *found elsewhere at this time). Dogberry, however, takes up the most literal interpretation.*

[21] And write 'God' first *His own concern with priority naturally makes him fussy about this kind of detail; an absurdity.*

defend but *forbid that*

[22] before *(for* after*)*

[22–3] it is proved already *Scarcely correct legal procedure, to begin by asserting the proof!*

[24] it will . . . shortly *everyone will think so soon*

[26] are none *are not (false knaves)*

[28–9] I will go about with him *I will get the better of him (he treats it as a matter of personal point-scoring)*

[29–30] Come . . . sir *His tone becomes more arrogant as he tries again.*

Scene 2. *Enter* DOGBERRY, VERGES, *and the* SEXTON (*in gowns*), *the* WATCH, CONRADE *and* BORACHIO

DOGBERRY Is our whole dissembly appeared?

VERGES O, a stool and a cushion for the Sexton.

SEXTON Which be the malefactors?

DOGBERRY Marry, that am I, and my partner.

VERGES Nay, that's certain; we have the exhibition to examine.

SEXTON But which are the offenders that are to be examined? Let them come before Master Constable.

DOGBERRY Yea, marry, let them come before me. 10 What is your name, friend?

BORACHIO Borachio.

DOGBERRY Pray write down, 'Borachio'. Yours, sirrah?

CONRADE I am a gentleman, sir, and my name is Conrade.

DOGBERRY Write down, 'Master Gentleman Conrade'. Masters, do you serve God?

CONRADE *and* ⎫
BORACHIO ⎬ Yea, sir, we hope.

DOGBERRY Write down that they hope they serve 20 God. And write 'God' first, for God defend but God should go before such villains! Masters, it is proved already that you are little better than false knaves, and it will go near to be thought so shortly. How answer you for yourselves?

CONRADE Marry, sir, we say we are none.

DOGBERRY [*Aside, to* VERGES *and the* SEXTON] A marvellous witty fellow, I assure you, but I will go about with him. [*Aloud*] Come you hither, sirrah; a

[33] Well, stand aside   *Having made an assertion rather than asked a question, he is stumped by their straight counter-assertion.*

'Fore   *before*

[34] tale   *conspiracy*

[36–7] you ... examine   *you're not going about the questioning in the right way*

[39] eftest   *most convenient*

[41] accuse   *make your charges against*

[44] Write ... villain   *Dogberry now in total confusion abbreviates the evidence, and then finds that the record amounts to a dangerous statement!*

[45] flat perjury   *an absolute lie*

[47–8] I do not like thy look   *He is irrelevantly personal again.*

[53] flat burglary   *Now that the main point of the evidence is reached, Dogberry focuses on the wrong aspect.*

[54] by mass   *by the mass (a common oath)*

[56–7] mean upon his words   *intend as a result of Borachio's evidence*

[60] redemption   *(for* damnation!*)*

word in your ear, sir. I say to you, it is thought you 30
are false knaves.

BORACHIO Sir, I say to you, we are none.

DOGBERRY Well, stand aside. 'Fore God, they are
both in a tale. Have you writ down that they are
none?

SEXTON Master Constable, you go not the way to
examine; you must call forth the watch that are
their accusers.

DOGBERRY Yea, marry, that's the eftest way. Let the
watch come forth. Masters, I charge you, in the 40
Prince's name, accuse these men.

FIRST WATCH This man said, sir, that Don John the
Prince's brother, was a villain.

DOGBERRY Write down, 'Prince John a villain'. Why,
this is flat perjury, to call a Prince's brother villain.

BORACHIO Master Constable –

DOGBERRY Pray thee, fellow, peace. I do not like thy
look, I promise thee.

SEXTON What heard you him say else?

SECOND WATCH Marry, that he had received a 50
thousand ducats of Don John for accusing the Lady
Hero wrongfully.

DOGBERRY Flat burglary as ever was committed.

VERGES Yea, by mass, that it is.

SEXTON What else, fellow?

FIRST WATCH And that Count Claudio did mean,
upon his words, to disgrace Hero before the whole
assembly, and not marry her.

DOGBERRY O villain – thou wilt be condemned into
everlasting redemption for this!   60

SEXTON What else?

SECOND WATCH This is all.

[64] Prince John . . . away   *The first news of this to the audience, which promises well for a speedy resolution. We can assume that he has fled on the news of Borachio's and Conrade's arrest.*

[66] upon   *as a result of*

[67] bound   *This is in the legal sense of 'bound over', but Dogberry takes it literally.*

[70] opinioned   *(for pinioned; held by the arms, like common criminals)*

[71] in the hands   *Verges' echo insults them further, as Conrade's response (as a gentleman) quickly demonstrates.*

[72] coxcomb   *fool (literally, the cap worn by the fool, shaped like a cock's comb)*

[73] God's my life   *as God is my life (an oath, expressing his amazement at Conrade's disrespect!)*

[75] naughty   *wicked*

[77] suspect   *(for respect. Conrade would of course be justified in suspecting Dogberry's ability as a constable.)*

[79] remember   *i.e. retain as evidence. Poor Dogberry unwittingly indicts himself still further.*

[82] piety   *(for impiety: irreverence)*

[83–90] I am a wise . . . ass   *From here to the end of his speech he is concerned to prove his worth; in doing so he exhibits his conceits and his insecurities, and reflects the values of the society around him.*

[86] go to   *i.e. I'll have you know*

[87–8] that hath had losses   *This is said as a matter of pride in his wealth, when in fact it shows he has made some bad decisions.*

[88] two gowns   *A valid boast, since a gown was quite costly.*

[90] O that I had been writ down   *would that it had been recorded*

SEXTON And this is more, masters, than you can deny.
  Prince John is this morning secretly stolen away;
  Hero was in this manner accused, in this very
  manner refused, and upon the grief of this suddenly
  died. Master Constable, let these men be bound
  and brought to Leonato's. I will go before and show
  him their examination.

[*Exit*

DOGBERRY Come, let them be opinioned.   70
VERGES Let them be – in the hands.
CONRADE Off, coxcomb!
DOGBERRY God's my life, where's the Sexton? Let
  him write down the Prince's officer 'coxcomb'.
  Come, bind them. Thou naughty varlet!
CONRADE Away – you are an ass, you are an ass!
DOGBERRY Dost thou not suspect my place? Dost thou
  not suspect my years? O that he were here, to write
  me down 'an ass'! But masters, remember that I am
  'an ass', though it be not written down, yet forget   80
  not that I am 'an ass'. No, thou villain, thou art full
  of piety, as shall be proved upon thee by good
  witness. I am a wise fellow; and, which is more, an
  officer; and, which is more, a householder; and,
  which is more, as pretty a piece of flesh as any is in
  Messina; and one that knows the law, go to; and a
  rich fellow enough, go to; and a fellow that hath
  had losses; and one that hath two gowns, and
  everything handsome about him. Bring him away.
  O that I had been writ down 'an ass'!   90

[*Exeunt*

ACT FIVE, scene 1

At last the effects of the arrest are going to be felt; but not before Leonato's distress has been accentuated, nor before Don Pedro and Claudio have been further revealed by their reactions to him, and by their attempted levity with Benedick. Both aspects serve to intensify the moment of realisation, which in turn asks important questions about the nature of culpability. After this Leonato takes control, arranging the conditions for the final practice. The scene probably takes place outside Leonato's house, which gives a theatrical echo of I. I.

[1] kill   *This recalls Borachio's prediction at II.2.29.*

[2] to second   *to back-up (literally: to act as a second, as in a duel)*

[3] counsel   *advice*

[6] Nor let no   *An elaborate double negative for emphasis.*

[7] suit with   *match*

[8] that so loved   *who loved (his child) in the same way*

[10] And bid him speak   *(with the emphasis falling on* him*)* *Leonato is saying that the only person he will take advice from is someone who has suffered in the same way as himself.*

[11] Measure his woe   *compare his sorrow with*

[12] answer every strain for strain   *correspond in every detail. A musical metaphor, in which* strain *means tune, and* answer, *to sing responses as in church music.*

[14] lineament   *feature*

[15] will smile, and stroke his beard   *i.e. behave casually*

[16] And sorrow, wag   *and wave misery on its way*

[17] Patch grief with proverbs   *mend his sorrow with quoting proverbs*

[17–18] make misfortune drunk/With candle-wasters   *i.e. drown his sorrows with philosophy;* candle-wasters: *the burners of midnight-oil, i.e. proverbially scholars, philosophers*

[18] yet   *even so*

[19] of   *from*

[22] not   *do not*

tasting it   *i.e. when they experience it*

[23–4] which . . . rage   *when they used to offer wise sayings to cure such anguish*

ACT FIVE

ANTONIO If you go on thus, you will kill yourself,
   And 'tis not wisdom thus to second grief
   Against yourself.
LEONATO   I pray thee cease thy counsel,
   Which falls into mine ears as profitless
   As water in a sieve. Give not me counsel,
   Nor let no comforter delight mine ear
   But such a one whose wrongs do suit with mine.
   Bring me a father that so loved his child,
   Whose joy of her is overwhelmed like mine,
   And bid him speak of patience.   10
   Measure his woe the length and breadth of
    mine,
   And let it answer every strain for strain,
   As thus for thus, and such a grief for such,
   In every lineament, branch, shape and form.
   If such a one will smile, and stroke his beard,
   And sorrow, wag, cry 'hem' when he should
    groan,
   Patch grief with proverbs, make misfortune
    drunk
   With candle-wasters – bring him yet to me
   And I of him will gather patience.
   But there is no such man; for brother, men 20
   Can counsel and speak comfort to that grief
   Which they themselves not feel; but tasting it,
   Their counsel turns to passion, which before
   Would give preceptial medicine to rage,

[25] Fetter strong madness in a silken thread   *i.e. restrain violent passion with feeble words of advice*

[26] Charm ache with air and agony with words   *attempt to soothe pain and suffering with the emptiness of words*

[27] 'tis all men's office   *everyone thinks it's his duty*

[28] wring under the load   *writhe under the burden*

[30] to be so moral   *i.e. to be able to take his own advice*

[32] my griefs cry louder than advertisement   *(1) (literal) no advice can be heard above my misery (2) all consolation is lost in the strength of my distress*

[34] I will be flesh and blood   *I can't help being human*

[35] there . . . philosopher   *there has yet to be a philosopher*

[37-8] However . . . sufferance   *however much they have succeeded in writing with elevated assurance and been quite contemptuous about the dealings of fate*

[39] bend not all the harm upon yourself   *i.e. don't take all the suffering on yourself; bend: aim, a metaphor from archery*

[42] belied   *slandered (the Sexton has not yet brought the truth)*

[46] Good den   *A shortened form of 'God give you good even'.*

Fetter strong madness in a silken thread,
Charm ache with air and agony with words.
No, no; 'tis all men's office to speak patience
To those that wring under the load of sorrow,
But no man's virtue nor sufficiency
To be so moral when he shall endure   30
The like himself. Therefore give me no counsel;
My griefs cry louder than advertisement.

ANTONIO Therein do men from children nothing
    differ.

LEONATO I pray thee, peace. I will be flesh and
    blood,
For there was never yet philosopher
That could endure the toothache patiently,
However they have writ the style of gods
And made a push at chance and sufferance.

ANTONIO Yet bend not all the harm upon yourself;
    Make those that do offend you suffer too.   40

LEONATO There thou speak'st reason. Nay, I will do
    so.
My soul doth tell me Hero is belied;
And that shall Claudio know, so shall the
    Prince,
And all of them that thus dishonour her.

Enter DON PEDRO *and* CLAUDIO

ANTONIO Here comes the Prince and Claudio
    hastily.

DON PEDRO Good den, good den.

CLAUDIO   Good day to both of you.

LEONATO Hear you, my lords –

DON PEDRO   We have some haste, Leonato.
                They do not stop

[49] **Are you so hasty now** *Leonato implies that previously they had all the time in the world; see I.1.147.*

all is one *it's neither here nor there (now). The tone is undoubtedly bitter.*

[53] **thou dissembler** *you hypocrite (note the change to the formal thou here)*

[55] **beshrew** *curse*

[56] **if it should give your age** *Claudio, whose hand has automatically reached for his sword, tries to extricate himself. He retains the 'you' form throughout.*

[57] **In faith . . . sword** *I assure you, my hand moved towards my sword quite unintentionally. Is Claudio exaggerating his innocence to make Leonato look foolish, or is he accidentally insulting?*

[58] **fleer** *sneer*

[59] **dotard** *senile old man*

[60] **As under privilege of age to brag** *taking the cover of seniority to boast (i.e. not able to be challenged)*

[62] **to thy head** *face to face*

[64] **to lay my reverence by** *to put aside the fact of my age, along with all the respect and immunity it affords me*

[65] **bruise** *A good word for conveying the sense of his long experience of life.*

[66] **trial of a man** *i.e. trial by equal combat*

[68] **through and through her heart** *(as though she has been stabbed, or run through with a sword)*

[71] **framed** *shaped (the first direct accusation) (for framed, compare I.3.24 and IV.1.188.)*

LEONATO Some haste, my lord? Well, fare you well,
    my lord.
    Are you so hasty now? Well, all is one.

DON PEDRO [*Returning*] Nay, do not quarrel with us,
    good old man.   50

ANTONIO If he could right himself with quarrelling
    Some of us would lie low.   Who wrongs him?

CLAUDIO

LEONATO Marry, thou dost wrong me, thou
    dissembler, thou!
    Nay, never lay hand upon thy sword;
    I fear thee not.

CLAUDIO   Marry, beshrew my hand
    If it should give your age such cause of fear.
    In faith, my hand meant nothing to my sword.

LEONATO Tush, tush, man, never fleer and jest at
    me.
    I speak not like a dotard nor a fool,
    As under privilege of age to brag   60
    What I have done being young, or what would
      do
    Were I not old. Know, Claudio, to thy head,
    Thou hast so wronged mine innocent child and
      me
    That I am forced to lay my reverence by,
    And with grey hairs and bruise of many days,
    Do challenge thee to trial of a man.
    I say thou hast belied mine innocent child.
    Thy slander hath gone through and through
      her heart,
    And she lies buried with her ancestors –
    O, in a tomb where never scandal slept,   70
    Save this of hers, framed by thy villainy!

[74] prove it on his body   *i.e. by fighting him*

[75] nice fence   *expertise with the sword (although Claudio has all the advantages of skill and current training, Leonato is still not afraid to challenge him)*

[76] May of youth   *May was the season traditionally symbolic of youth, energy, physical prowess and so on.*

lustihood   *physical fitness*

[77] I will not have to do with you   *I don't wish to fight you*

[78] daff   *put me aside (from do + off)*

[79] boy   *This is intentionally insulting, as taken up by Antonio.*

[80–5] He shall ... I will   *The strength of Antonio's sudden intervention takes everyone by surprise; even Leonato cannot restrain his ardour. The spectacle of his frenzied verbal attack on the younger man contains much that is absurd; but within the intensity of the dramatic context the absurdity is balanced by his real sense of outrage.*

[82] Win me and wear me   *defeat me and make the victory public; wear refers to the tradition in which the victor displayed the colours or tokens of the defeated*

[83] Come, follow me, boy   *He is being as taunting and insulting as he can be.*

[84] I'll whip ... fence   *i.e. he'll give him some real fighting to think about, instead of mere show (also grossly insulting); foining: thrusting (a term in fencing)*

[87] Content yourself   *Be quiet*

[89–90] That dare ... tongue   *He is implying that they will certainly need courage to take him on.*

[91] apes ... milk-sops   *imitators, boasters, knaves, feeble boys*

[92] Hold you content   *Again, Antonio won't be stopped.*

[93] what they weigh   *what they are worth*

[94] Scambling, out-facing, fashion-monging   *brawling, swaggering, fashion-conscious*

[95] cog and flout, deprave   *cheat and mock, vilify*

CLAUDIO My villainy?

LEONATO   Thine, Claudio, thine, I say.

DON PEDRO You say not right, old man.

LEONATO   My lord, my lord,
   I'll prove it on his body if he dare,
   Despite his nice fence and his active practice,
   His May of youth and bloom of lustihood.

CLAUDIO Away; I will not have to do with you.

LEONATO Canst thou so daff me? Thou hast killed
   my child;
   If thou kill'st me, boy, thou shalt kill a man.

ANTONIO He shall kill two of us and men indeed.   80
   But that's no matter; let him kill one first.
   Win me and wear me, let him answer me.
   Come, follow me, boy, come, sir boy, come
   follow me
   Sir boy, I'll whip you from your foining fence;
   Nay, as I am a gentleman, I will.

LEONATO Brother –

ANTONIO Content yourself. God knows, I loved my
   niece;
   And she is dead, slandered to death by villains,
   That dare as well answer a man indeed
   As I dare take a serpent by the tongue.   90
   Boys, apes, braggarts, Jacks, milk-sops!

LEONATO   Brother Antony –

ANTONIO Hold you content. What, man! I know
   them, yea,
   And what they weigh, even to the utmost
   scruple –
   Scambling, outfacing, fashion-monging boys,
   That lie and cog and flout, deprave and
   slander,

[96] Go anticly   *behave like idiots (literally, like an antic or buffoon)*

[96–98] show outward ... durst   *i.e. make a great show of how fierce and aggressive they could be, if they chose*

[102] we will not wake your patience   *we won't ask you to be patient (since that would make things worse)*

[105] full of proof   *absolutely proved*

[113–14] you are ... fray   *you've just missed having to part the sides in what was just about to be a fight. Despite the gravity of feeling expressed by Leonato and Antonio, Don Pedro can still manage this verbal play.*

[115] had liked to have   *were about to have*

[116] with   *by*

[118] doubt   *suspect (ironical)*

Go anticly and show outward hideousness,
And speak off half a dozen dangerous words
How they might hurt their enemies, if they
    durst;
And this is all.

LEONATO But, brother Antony –

ANTONIO   Come, 'tis no matter 100
Do not you meddle, let me deal in this.

DON PEDRO Gentlemen both, we will not wake your
    patience;
My heart is sorry for your daughter's death,
But on my honour she was charged with
    nothing
But what was true, and very full of proof.

LEONATO My lord, my lord –

DON PEDRO I will not hear you.

LEONATO No? Come, brother, away; I will be
    heard.

ANTONIO And shall, or some of us will smart for it.

            [*Exeunt* LEONATO *and* ANTONIO

Enter BENEDICK

DON PEDRO See, see, here comes the man we went to
    seek.   110

CLAUDIO Now, signor, what news?

BENEDICK Good day, my lord.

DON PEDRO Welcome, signor; you are almost come to
part almost a fray.

CLAUDIO We had like to have had our two noses
snapped off with two old men without teeth –

DON PEDRO Leonato and his brother. What think'st
thou? Had we fought, I doubt we should have been
too young for them.

[122] up and down to seek thee   *looking for you everywhere*

[123] high-proof melancholy   *extremely depressed*

[123–4] would fain have it beaten away   *i.e. would very much like some kind of distraction (such as Benedick's wit can usually provide)*

[125] It is in my scabbard   *Benedick intends to provide that distraction, in the form of his sword/challenge.*

[127] Never any   *no one ever*

[128] beside their wit   *mad. Claudio reverses Don Pedro's notion of wit being worn at the side like a sword.*

draw   *(1) take out of its case (appropriate for either sword or musical instrument) (2) draw a bow across the strings (also bawdy)*

[130–1] As I am . . . angry   *Don Pedro begins to realise that Benedick is serious.*

[132–3] care killed a cat   *A proverbial saying, meaning that worry can't kill people; and a derogatory reference to Hero?*

[133] mettle   *resilient spirit*

[135] meet . . . the career   *answer your wit at full charge. The metaphor is from jousting (tilting), in which two horsemen with lances ride at full speed towards one another.* career: *charge*

[138–9] Nay then . . . cross   *(Claudio continues the metaphor) For the lance to be broken across the body of the other contestant was considered poor tilting; Claudio is implying that Benedick's wit isn't up to much and recommends another staff.*

[141] indeed   *i.e. actually, and not just pretending*

[142] he knows how to turn his girdle   *A saying with the general meaning of 'He knows what to do about it'; possibly from wrestling, where belts were turned with the buckle to the back when preparing for a fight.*

[143] in your ear   *privately (out of Don Pedro's hearing)*

[144] bless   *keep*

[146] make it good   *prove it*

[146–7] how you dare . . . you dare   *how, when and with whatever weapons you choose (dare echoes Claudio's scathing exclamations to Leonato at IV.1.18)*

[147] Do me right   *give me satisfaction*

[148] protest   *publicly proclaim*

[150] hear from you   *have a response (formal, to the challenge)*

[151–2] good cheer   *friendly hospitality. Either he is being ironical, or he is still treating Benedick lightly. There is also a pun on meet/meat.*

BENEDICK In a false quarrel there is no true valour. 120
    I came to seek you both.

CLAUDIO We have been up and down to seek thee, for
    we are high-proof melancholy and would fain have
    it beaten away. Wilt thou use thy wit?

BENEDICK It is in my scabbard – shall I draw it?

DON PEDRO Dost thou wear thy wit by thy side?

CLAUDIO Never any did so, though very many have
    been beside their wit. I will bid thee draw, as we do
    the minstrels: draw to pleasure us.

DON PEDRO As I am an honest man, he looks pale. Art 130
    thou sick, or angry?

CLAUDIO What? Courage, man. What though care
    killed a cat; thou hast mettle enough in thee to kill
    care.

BENEDICK Sir, I shall meet your wit in the career, an
    you charge it against me. I pray you, choose
    another subject.

CLAUDIO Nay then, give him another staff; this last
    was broke cross.

DON PEDRO By this light, he changes more and more. 140
    I think he be angry indeed.

CLAUDIO If he be, he knows how to turn his girdle.

BENEDICK Shall I speak a word in your ear?

CLAUDIO God bless me from a challenge!

BENEDICK [Aside to CLAUDIO] You are a villain; I jest
    not. I will make it good how you dare, with what
    you dare, and when you dare. Do me right, or I will
    protest your cowardice. You have killed a sweet
    lady, and her death shall fall heavy on you. Let me
    hear from you. 150

CLAUDIO Well, I will meet you, so I may have good
    cheer.

[153] a feast, a feast   *Don Pedro picks up on* cheer *with enthusiasm, hoping for a social event to relieve the tension.*

[154–7] He hath . . . woodcock too   *Each item of food in this 'feast' represents foolishness. Claudio implies that Benedick's challenge is idiotic.*

[155] calf's head   *fool*
capon   *stupid person (abusive term – literally, a neutered cock)*

[155–6] carve most curiously   *(1) cut up very skilfully, or (2) fight well*

[156] knife   *(1) carving knife, or (2) sword*
naught   *useless*

[157] woodcock   *Considered a foolish bird because it was easy to catch.*

[158] ambles well; it goes easily   *Benedick retaliates by comparing the rate of Claudio's wit to a slow-plodding horse.*

[159–72] I'll tell . . . Italy   *The whole speech attempts to avert the seriousness of Benedick's mood, ignorant of the declarations of love between Beatrice and Benedick (at IV. 1).*

[160] fine   *delicate*

[163] Just   *exactly*

[165] hath the tongues   *knows foreign languages*

[169] trans-shape   *distort*

[171] properest   *most handsome*

[176] deadly   *mortally*

[177] the old man's daughter   *i.e. Hero. He seems unable to use her name; what a contrast to his 'gentle Hero' at II.1.367).*

[178–9] God . . . garden   *A reference to the story (Genesis 3) of Adam in Eden, who tried to hide from God. Benedick in the orchard thought himself unobserved (II. 3).*

[180–81] But when . . . head   *when will Benedick become eligible to be made a cuckold (i.e. when will he be married). Don Pedro is reminding him of his boast at I.1.257.*

DON PEDRO What, a feast, a feast?

CLAUDIO I'faith I thank him. He hath bid me to a calf's head and a capon, the which, if I do not carve most curiously, say my knife's naught. Shall I not find a woodcock too?

BENEDICK Sir, your wit ambles well; it goes easily.

DON PEDRO I'll tell thee how Beatrice praised thy wit the other day. I said thou hadst a fine wit. 'True,' 160 said she, 'a fine little one.' 'No,' said I, 'a great wit.' 'Right,' says she, 'a great gross one.' 'Nay,' said I, 'a good wit.' 'Just,' said she, 'it hurts nobody!' 'Nay,' said I, 'the gentleman is wise.' 'Certain,' said she, 'a wise gentleman.' 'Nay,' said I, 'he hath the tongues.' 'That I believe,' said she, 'for he swore a thing to me on Monday night, which he forswore on Tuesday morning – there's a double tongue, there's two tongues.' Thus did she, an hour together, trans-shape thy particular virtues; yet at last she 170 concluded with a sigh, thou wast the properest man in Italy.

CLAUDIO For the which she wept heartily, and said she cared not.

DON PEDRO Yea, that she did. But yet for all that, an if she did not hate him deadly, she would love him dearly; the old man's daughter told us all.

CLAUDIO All, all; and moreover, God saw him when he was hid in the garden.

DON PEDRO But when shall we set the savage bull's 180 horns on the sensible Benedick's head?

CLAUDIO Yea, and text underneath, 'Here dwells Benedick, the married man'?

BENEDICK Fare you well, boy; you know my mind. I will leave you now to your gossip-like humour. You

[186] as braggarts do their blades   *as those who boast of fencing skill but do not show it*

[191] Lord Lackbeard   *Another insult, like 'boy'.*
[192] shall meet. *i.e. for the challenge*

[199] pretty   *fine (ironical)*
[199–200] when he . . . wit   *walks about without the covering of his intelligence (*wit *is being equated with a cloak here)*
[201–2] He is then . . . man   *although he might look like a hero when compared with a fool, compared to a man in this state, even a fool is wiser (*Ape *could also be taken literally.)*
[203] soft you, let me be   *The implications of Benedick's news begin to sink in.*
[203–4] pluck up, my heart   *rouse yourself*
[204] sad   *serious*
[207] she shall . . . balance   *The image of the scales of justice is confused with domestic scales—one weighs reasons (from the French,* raison*) and the other,* raisins.
[208] an   *if*
once   *i.e. positively*
[212] Hearken after   *find out*

break jests as braggarts do their blades – which God
be thanked hurt not. [*To* DON PEDRO] My lord, for
your many courtesies I thank you; I must discon-
tinue your company. Your brother the Bastard is
fled from Messina. You have among you killed a 190
sweet and innocent lady. For my Lord Lackbeard
there, he and I shall meet; and till then, peace be
with him.

[*Exit*

DON PEDRO He is in earnest.

CLAUDIO In most profound earnest, and I'll warrant
you, for the love of Beatrice.

DON PEDRO And hath challenged thee?

CLAUDIO Most sincerely.

DON PEDRO What a pretty thing man is, when he goes
in his doublet and hose and leaves off his wit! 200

CLAUDIO He is then a giant to an ape; but then is an
ape a doctor to such a man.

DON PEDRO But soft you, let me be; pluck up, my
heart, and be sad. Did he not say my brother was
fled?

Enter DOGBERRY, VERGES, CONRADE *and* BORACHIO *with
the* WATCH

DOGBERRY Come you, sir. If justice cannot tame you,
she shall ne'er weigh more reasons in her balance.
Nay, an you be a cursing hypocrite once, you must
be looked to.

DON PEDRO How now? Two of my brother's men 210
bound – Borachio one?

CLAUDIO Hearken after their offence, my lord.

DON PEDRO Officers, what offence have these men
done?

193

[215–20] Marry sir . . . knaves *Each of Dogberry's accusations is of course saying the same thing – a fact which Don Pedro is quick to imitate in his reply.*

[215–16] committed false report *given false testimony*

[217] secondarily *(for* secondly*)*

slanders *(for* slanderers*)*

[218] belied *misrepresented*

[225] his own division *using the same numbering*

[226] well-suited *i.e. dressed in several different ways*

[228] bound to your answer *legally bound to answer to the charges*

[229] cunning *clever*

[231] go no farther to mine answer *wait no longer before telling you*

[232] Do you *i.e. please*

[233–5] What . . . light *An humiliating irony.*

[237] incensed *incited*

[239] in Hero's garments *The first time we have heard this detail of the plot.*

[240] should marry *should have married*

[242] seal *i.e. finish off*

[246] Runs not . . . blood *The intense horror expressed here and in Claudio's reply needs no elaboration. Claudio's image recalls Borachio at II.2.21, and Hero at III.1.86. (Note the change to verse here.)*

DOGBERRY Marry, sir, they have committed false
report; moreover, they have spoken untruths;
secondarily, they are slanders; sixth and lastly, they
have belied a lady; thirdly, they have verified
unjust things; and, to conclude, they are lying
knaves.   220

DON PEDRO First, I ask thee what they have done;
thirdly, I ask thee, what's their offence; sixth and
lastly, why they are committed; and, to conclude,
what you lay to their charge?

CLAUDIO Rightly reasoned, and in his own division;
and by my troth there's one meaning well-suited.

DON PEDRO Who have you offended, masters, that you
are thus bound to your answer? This learned
Constable is too cunning to be understood. What's
your offence?   230

BORACHIO Sweet Prince, let me go no farther to mine
answer. Do you hear me and let this Count kill me. I
have deceived even your very eyes. What your
wisdoms could not discover, these shallow fools
have brought to light; who in the night overheard
me confessing to this man, how Don John, your
brother, incensed me to slander the Lady Hero;
how you were brought into the orchard and saw me
court Margaret in Hero's garments; how you
disgraced her when you should marry her. My 240
villainy they have upon record, which I had rather
seal with my death than repeat over to my shame.
The lady is dead upon mine and my master's false
accusation. And briefly, I desire nothing but the
reward of a villain.

DON PEDRO Runs not this speech like iron through
        your blood?

[254] plaintiffs *He means defendants.*
[255] reformed *(for informed)*
[257] shall serve *provide an opportunity*
that I am an ass *As before (IV.2.77–90) he is still concerned to get the records straight!*

[263] would *want to*
[264] breath *words*
[266] beliest *give false testimony about*

[271] if you bethink you of it *if you think about it (heavily sarcastic)*

CLAUDIO I have drunk poison whiles he uttered it.

DON PEDRO But did my brother set thee on to this?

BORACHIO Yea, and paid me richly for the practice
     of it.

DON PEDRO He is composed and framed of
     treachery.   250
     And fled he is upon this villainy.

CLAUDIO Sweet Hero, now thy image doth appear
     In the rare semblance that I loved it first.

DOGBERRY Come, bring away the plaintiffs; by this
    time our Sexton hath reformed Signor Leonato of
    the matter. And masters, do not forget to specify,
    when time and place shall serve, that I am an ass.

VERGES Here, here comes master Signor Leonato, and
    the Sexton too.

Enter LEONATO, ANTONIO *and the* SEXTON

LEONATO Which is the villain? Let me see his eyes   260
     That when I note another man like him
     I may avoid him. Which of these is he?

BORACHIO If you would know your wronger, look on
     me.

LEONATO Art thou the slave that with thy breath
     hast killed
     Mine innocent child?

BORACHIO   Yea, even I alone.

LEONATO No, not so, villain, thou beliest thyself.
     Here stand a pair of honourable men,
     A third is fled, that had a hand in it.
     I thank you, Princes, for my daughter's death,
     Record it with your high and worthy deeds.   270
     'Twas bravely done, if you bethink you of it.

CLAUDIO I know not how to pray your patience,

[274] Impose me to   *impose on me*
invention   *ingenuity*
[275–6] Yet sinned I not/But in mistaking   *Crucial in the play is this idea of 'culpable credulity' (see Introduction, p. 10). How justifiable is Claudio's statement?*
[277] this good old man   *Rather different from their attitude earlier in the scene.*
[279] That he'll enjoin me to   *that he requires of me*
[282] possess   *inform*
[283–4] if . . . invention   *if you're able to create anything from what you feel for her*
[286] sing it tonight   *Leonato wants of course to put Claudio quickly through that process, in order to move on to the next stage.*

[289] a daughter   *Invented for the purpose; it is feasible that Claudio could be unaware of her existence.*
[291] she alone is heir   *He seems to give Claudio plenty of inducement to comply.*

[295–6] and dispose/For henceforth   *From duelling; if the winner spared the life of his opponent, it remained at his 'disposal'.*
[297] expect   *wait for*
[298] naughty   *wicked*

Yet I must speak. Choose your revenge
    yourself;
Impose me to what penance your invention
Can lay upon my sin; yet sinned I not
But in mistaking.

DON PEDRO   By my soul, nor I.
And yet, to satisfy this good old man,
I would bend under any heavy weight
That he'll enjoin me to.

LEONATO I cannot bid you bid my daughter live,   280
That were impossible. But I pray you both,
Possess the people in Messina here
How innocent she died; and if your love
Can labour aught in sad invention,
Hang her an epitaph upon her tomb
And sing it to her bones, sing it tonight.
Tomorrow morning, come you to my house;
And since you could not be my son-in-law,
Be yet my nephew. My brother hath a
    daughter
Almost the copy of my child that's dead,   290
And she alone is heir to both of us.
Give her the right you should have giv'n her
    cousin,
And so dies my revenge.

CLAUDIO   O noble sir,
Your over-kindness doth wring tears from me.
I do embrace your offer, and dispose
For henceforth of poor Claudio.

LEONATO Tomorrow then, I will expect your
    coming;
Tonight I take my leave. This naughty man
Shall face to face be brought to Margaret,

[300] packed   *knowingly involved*
[304] by her   *about her*
[305–6] under white and black   *in writing*

[309] one Deformed   *From the Watchman's misunderstanding of 'deformed thief' at III.3. Dogberry improves on the report with details of his own.*

[311] in God's name   *Either, on the basis of an oath, or literally, borrowing as though for a religious purpose.*

[312–14] the which ... sake   *Does Dogberry have first-hand experience of this problem?*

[312] paid   *repaid*

[317–18] most thankful and reverend youth   *(a characteristic confusion)*

[320] God save the foundation   *Dogberry gives thanks as though for having received charity from a religious organisation – either a typical mistake; or a revealing slip of the tongue, suggesting the source of his income?*

[321] discharge   *Leonato officially relieves him of his responsibilities.*

[324] to correct yourself   *He is asking Leonato to supervise the punishment himself but it is unfortunately expressed.*

[327] give   *(for ask)*

[328] prohibit   *(for protect or promote)*

Who I believe was packed in all this wrong,   300
Hired to it by your brother.

BORACHIO   No, by my soul, she was not;
Nor knew not what she did when she spoke to
   me,
But always hath been just and virtuous
In anything that I do know by her.

DOGBERRY Moreover, sir, which indeed is not under white and black, this plaintiff here, the offender, did call me ass. I beseech you, let it be remembered in his punishment. And also, the watch heard them talk of one Deformed – they say he wears a key in his ear and a lock hanging 310 by it, and borrows money in God's name, the which he hath used so long and never paid, that now men grow hard-hearted and will lend nothing for God's sake. Pray you, examine him upon that point.

LEONATO I thank thee for thy care and honest
   pains.

DOGBERRY Your worship speaks like a most thankful and reverend youth, and I praise God for you.

LEONATO There's for thy pains. [*He gives him money*]

DOGBERRY God save the foundation!   320

LEONATO Go, I discharge thee of thy prisoner, and I thank thee.

DOGBERRY I leave an arrant knave with your worship, which I beseech your worship to correct yourself for the example of others. God keep your worship, I wish your worship well. God restore you to health; I humbly give you leave to depart, and if a merry meeting may be wished, God prohibit it! Come, neighbour.

[332] with Hero   *i.e. at her tomb*
[334] lewd   *base*

ACT FIVE, scene 2

Although still unaware of the revealed truth, Beatrice and Benedick reflect a lightening of the atmosphere in the return of their witty exchange. They meet somewhere outside Leonato's house; the best location would be the garden where their loves were first 'shown' to them.

[1–2] deserve . . . hands   *earn my thanks*
[2] to the speech of   *to have conversation with*
[6]· so high a style   *such elaborate style (with a pun on style/stile)*
[7] come over   *(1) write better (2) climb over*
comely   *good-looking*
[9] come over me   *She means sexually.*
[10] below stairs   *as a servant (and never become a mistress either of house or husband)*
[12] it catches   *i.e. it's like a snare (also with bawdy implications). Benedick, like Beatrice earlier, seems taken by surprise at Margaret's mental agility.*
[13] foils   *light swords (made blunt for fencing)*
[15–16] A most . . . woman   *a suitably masculine brand of wit, which won't damage a woman*
[17] I give thee the bucklers   *Jokingly Benedick resigns the 'fight' to her.* bucklers: *small shields*

[*Exeunt* DOGBERRY *and* VERGES

LEONATO Until tomorrow morning, lords, farewell.   330

ANTONIO Farewell, my lords; we look for you
   tomorrow.

DON PEDRO We will not fail.

CLAUDIO   Tonight I'll mourn with Hero.

   [*Exeunt* DON PEDRO *and* CLAUDIO

LEONATO Bring you these fellows on. We'll talk with
   Margaret,

   How her acquaintance grew with this lewd
   fellow.

                    [*Exeunt*

Scene 2. *Enter* BENEDICK *and* MARGARET

BENEDICK Pray thee, sweet Mistress Margaret, deserve well at my hands by helping me to the speech
   of Beatrice.

MARGARET Will you then write me a sonnet in praise
   of my beauty?

BENEDICK In so high a style, Margaret, that no man
   living shall come over it, for in most comely truth
   thou deservest it.

MARGARET To have no man come over me! Why,
   shall I always keep below stairs?   10

BENEDICK Thy wit is as quick as the greyhound's
   mouth; it catches.

MARGARET And yours as blunt as the fencer's foils,
   which hit but hurt not.

BENEDICK A most manly wit, Margaret, it will not
   hurt a woman. And so I pray thee call Beatrice; I
   give thee the bucklers.

[18–19] Give us . . . own   *A bawdy response, in which the weapons represent male and female sexual organs.*

[21] pikes   *spikes which were put in the centre of the shield*

vice   *screw (with pikes; obviously bawdy)*

[22] maids   *virgins (even Margaret gives up after this joke)*

[25–41] And therefore . . . terms   *Benedick now attempts the role of ideal lover, both singing a love song and writing poetry; but the first peters out and the second fails. He concludes that it is not his style, thus retaining his image as the Anti-Lover intact.*

[26] The God of Love   *The beginning of an old song which would have been well-known.*

[30] Leander   *In the Greek legend, Leander swam the Hellespont to his lover, Hero (see IV.1.99).*

[31] Troilus   *The story of the tragic love of Troilus for Cressida is told by several authors, including Shakespeare; pandars comes from Pandarus, the go-between in the story.*

[32] quondam carpet-mongers   *former ladies-men. A carpet-knight was a man who stood more often on carpets than on the battlefield!*

[33] yet   *even so*

[35] turned over and over   *A pun with several possible sources: (1) given a rough ride (in contrast with those who 'run smoothly in the even road'); (2) turned in the sense of composed: they run smoothly in blank verse, he has been constantly rewritten; (3) like the pages of a book being thumbed through (from 'whole bookful'). Each conveys his sense of having been 'turned upside down' by love.*

as my poor self   *The standard egotism of the lover, who thinks his pain is worse than anybody else's.*

[37] innocent   *silly*

[39–40] ominous endings   *i.e. they don't promise well, either for versification or the furtherance of his love*

[40–1] a rhyming planet   *i.e. the stars' influence at his birth was not a poetic one*

[41] in festival terms   *in a style suitable for public rendering*

[46] 'Then' is spoken   *Beatrice is teasing him again.*

[47] with that I came   *with the knowledge I came for*

MARGARET Give us the swords; we have bucklers of
our own.

BENEDICK If you use them, Margaret, you must put in   20
the pikes with a vice; and they are dangerous
weapons for maids.

MARGARET Well, I will call Beatrice to you, who I
think hath legs.

[*Exit*

BENEDICK And therefore will come.

[*Sings*] The God of Love
That sits above,
And knows me, and knows me,
How pitiful I deserve –

I mean in singing. But in loving, Leander the good   30
swimmer, Troilus the first employer of pandars,
and a whole bookful of these quondam carpet-
mongers, whose names yet run smoothly in the even
road of a blank verse – why, they were never so truly
turned over and over as my poor self in love. Marry,
I cannot show it in rhyme – I have tried: I can find
out no rhyme to 'lady' but 'baby' – an innocent
rhyme; for 'scorn', 'horn' – a hard rhyme; for
'school', 'fool' – a babbling rhyme, very ominous
endings. No, I was not born under a rhyming   40
planet, nor I cannot woo in festival terms.

Enter BEATRICE

Sweet Beatrice, wouldst thou come when I called
thee?

BEATRICE Yea, signor, and depart when you bid me.

BENEDICK O stay but till then.

BEATRICE 'Then' is spoken; fare you well now. And
yet, ere I go, let me go with that I came – which is,

[53] noisome *revolting*

[55-6] Thou hast . . . sense *you've distorted my original meaning (of foul) completely*

[57] undergoes my challenge *has been challenged (for which a reply is awaited)*

[59] subscribe *proclaim (in writing)*

[63] so politic a state of evil *such a consistently wicked rule*

[65] suffer *(1) allow (2) endure*

[66] good epithet *good description (he takes* suffer *in the sense of endure)*

[68] In spite of your heart *despite your inclinations (she then uses* spite *more literally)*

[69-70] If you . . . hates *if you torment it on my behalf, I'll torment it on your behalf, because I'll never love what my lover hates*

[72] It appears . . . confession *i.e. your statement doesn't seem too wise*

[75] instance *example*

[75-6] that lived . . . neighbours *that was relevant when there were such things as good neighbours; a reference to the adage, 'He who praises himself has ill neighbours'.*

[76-9] If a man . . . weeps *these days, if you don't establish your own reputation before you die, your memory won't survive longer than the tolling of the funeral bell, or the tears of those left behind*

with knowing what hath passed between you and
Claudio.

BENEDICK Only foul words, and thereupon I will kiss 50
thee.

BEATRICE Foul words is but foul wind, and foul wind
is but foul breath, and foul breath is noisome –
therefore, I will depart unkissed.

BENEDICK Thou hast frighted the word out of his right
sense, so forcible is thy wit. But I must tell thee
plainly: Claudio undergoes my challenge, and
either I must shortly hear from him, or I will
subscribe him a coward. And I pray thee now tell
me, for which of my bad parts didst thou first fall in 60
love with me?

BEATRICE For them all together, which maintained so
politic a state of evil that they will not admit any
good part to intermingle with them. But for which
of my good parts did you first suffer love for me?

BENEDICK 'Suffer love'? A good epithet; I do suffer
love indeed, for I love thee against my will!

BEATRICE In spite of your heart, I think. Alas, poor
heart! If you spite it for my sake, I will spite it for
yours, for I will never love that which my friend 70
hates.

BENEDICK Thou and I are too wise to woo peaceably.

BEATRICE It appears not in the confession; there's not
one wise man among twenty that will praise
himself.

BENEDICK An old, an old instance, Beatrice, that lived
in the time of good neighbours. If a man do not
erect in this age his own tomb ere he dies, he shall
live no longer in monument than the bell rings and
the widow weeps. 80

[82] Question *i.e. that's a good question*
clamour *noise*
[83] rheum *tears*
[84] Don Worm, his conscience *The image of conscience as a worm or serpent occurs in the Bible and other writings.*
[85–6] the trumpet . . . virtues *i.e. the proclaimer of them (compare the expression 'blow one's own trumpet')*
[86] So much for *that's enough of*

[93] mend *put yourself to rights*
[96] yonder's old coil *there's total confusion*
[98–9] the author of all *the one responsible for it all*

[100] presently *immediately*
[102] die *(1) in opposition to 'live', and often at this time (2) a metaphor for sexual orgasm*
[103–4] be buried in thy eyes *i.e. by gazing into them*

ACT FIVE, scene 3

This scene directly contrasts with IV. 1 both in staging and in intention. The atmosphere is sombre, the stage sparsely populated; but while it seems brief in text (to some, indicative of Claudio's lack of feeling), in performance it becomes a solemn ritual of penance, which is necessary before the final practice can effect a restoration.

[with tapers] *i.e. carrying candles*
[1] monument *family tomb*

BEATRICE And how long is that, think you?

BENEDICK Question – why, an hour in clamour and a quarter in rheum. Therefore is it most expedient for the wise – if Don Worm, his conscience, find no impediment to the contrary – to be the trumpet of his own virtues, as I am to myself. So much for praising myself, who I myself will bear witness is praise-worthy. And now tell me, how doth your cousin?

BEATRICE Very ill. 90

BENEDICK And how do you?

BEATRICE Very ill too.

BENEDICK Serve God, love me, and mend. There will I leave you too, for here comes one in haste.

Enter URSULA

URSULA Madam, you must come to your uncle; yonder's old coil at home. It is proved my Lady Hero hath been falsely accused, the Prince and Claudio mightily abused and Don John is the author of all, who is fled and gone. Will you come presently? 100

BEATRICE Will you go hear this news, signor?

BENEDICK I will live in thy heart, die in thy lap, and be buried in thy eyes. And moreover, I will go with thee to thy uncle's.

[*Exeunt*

Scene 3. *Enter* CLAUDIO, DON PEDRO, BALTHASAR, *and three or four attendant lords, with tapers*

CLAUDIO Is this the monument of Leonato?

A LORD It is, my lord.

[Epitaph]   *This stresses that while she was killed through the destruction of her reputation, she now lives through the heroism of her innocent victimisation. An exaggeration which fits the convention.*

[5] guerdon   *recompense*

[8] with   *from*

[BALTHASAR sings]   *The singer was not in fact named by Shakespeare; most editors name him as here. The absolute solemnity of the song, and of Claudio's yearly commitment to remembrance, act as a release from tragic experience for him and for the play. The effect is immediate (see Don Pedro's speech at l. 24).*

[12] goddess of the night   *Diana, goddess of the moon, the patroness of virgins.*

[13] thy virgin knight   *Hero (as virgin) is characterised as an attendant to the goddess. (In the legend Hero was, by contrast, a nun of Venus. See also Claudio's description of her, at IV.1.56–60.)*

[19–20] Graves yawn ... utterèd   *i.e. may nothing be at peace until this death has been properly commemorated*

[24] Good morrow   *A sudden brightening in tone.*

[25] have preyed   *have finished hunting. There is also the symbolic sense – he and Claudio have finished 'preying on' Hero.*

the gentle day   *dawn, symbolising the 'new beginning'*

[26] Before   *in front of*

the wheels of Phoebus   *In Greek mythology the sun god, Phoebus, was thought to ride across the sky in a chariot.*

CLAUDIO [*Reading from a scroll*]

Epitaph
Done to death by slanderous tongues
　　Was the Hero that here lies.
Death, in guerdon of her wrongs,
　　Gives her fame which never dies.
So the life that died with shame
　　Lives in death with glorious fame.
Hang thou there upon the tomb
　　Praising her when I am dumb.　　　　　　10
[*He hangs the scroll on the tomb*]

Now music sound, and sing your solemn hymn.

BALTHASAR [*Sings*]

　　　Pardon, goddess of the night,
　　　Those that slew thy virgin knight,
　　　For the which with songs of woe
　　　Round about her tomb they go.
　　　Midnight assist our moan,
　　　Help us to sigh and groan,
　　　　　Heavily, heavily.
　　　Graves yawn and yield your dead,
　　　Till death be utterèd,　　　　　　20
　　　　　Heavily, heavily.

CLAUDIO　Now unto thy bones, good night;
　　　Yearly will I do this rite.
DON PEDRO　Good morrow, masters; put your torches
　　　out,
　　　The wolves have preyed, and look, the gentle
　　　day
　　　Before the wheels of Phoebus, round about

[29] several   *separate*
[30] weeds   *clothes*
[32] Hymen   *god of marriage*
issue   *outcome*
speed's   *bring us*
[33] for whom   *i.e. Hero*
this woe   *our lament*

ACT FIVE, scene 4

Finally, back inside Leonato's house where the first dance took place, Claudio faces the real test, which ironically insists on his taking a new bride at the 'face-value' of her deceptive mask. One last teasing hold-up in the other match is resolved so that the dance, literal and metaphorical, may proceed. On stage, this final spectacle is a perfect image for the hard-won unities.

[3] Upon   *on the basis of*
debated   *discussed*
[5] Although against her will   *This seems to conflict with Borachio's claim at V.1.301; but it could mean 'although unintentionally'.*
[7] sort   *turn out*
[8] by faith enforced   *compelled by keeping my word*
[9] reckoning   *payment (in the form of a duel) (See IV.1.334, 'Claudio shall render me a dear account'.)*
[12] masked   *It is now the women's turn to be masked.*
[14] office   *role*
[15] be   *pretend to be*

Dapples the drowsy east with spots of grey.
Thanks to you all, and leave us. Fare you well.
CLAUDIO Good morrow masters, each his several
    way.

                       [Exeunt attendants
DON PEDRO Come let us hence, and put on other
    weeds,   30
And then to Leonato's we will go.
CLAUDIO And Hymen now with luckier issue speed's
    Than this for whom we rendered up this woe.

                                    [Exeunt

Scene 4. *Enter* LEONATO, ANTONIO, BENEDICK, BEATRICE,
    HERO, MARGARET, URSULA, *and the* FRIAR

FRIAR Did I not tell you she was innocent?
LEONATO So are the Prince and Claudio, who
    accused her
Upon the error that you heard debated.
But Margaret was in some fault for this,
Although against her will, as it appears
In the true course of all the question.
ANTONIO Well, I am glad that all things sort so well.
BENEDICK And so am I, being else by faith enforced
    To call young Claudio to a reckoning for it.
LEONATO Well, daughter, and you gentlewomen all,   10
Withdraw into a chamber by yourselves,
And when I send for you come hither masked.
The Prince and Claudio promised by this hour
To visit me. You know your office, brother;
You must be father to your brother's daughter
And give her to young Claudio.

                      [Exeunt all the women

[17] with confirmed countenance   *keeping a straight face*

[18] entreat your pains   *beg to trouble you (not the usual confident speech of Benedick)*

[20] To bind me, or undo me   *Both would be possible through marriage, Benedick realises, and hence his hesitancy.*

[21] Signor Leonato . . . signor   *Again, an unusual nervousness!*

[23] lent her   *i.e. through the practice at III.1*

[24] requite her   *love her in return*

[25] the sight whereof   *Leonato refers to their tricking of him this time, at II.3, continuing the idea of the 'eye' of love.*

[27] enigmatical   *obscure. Benedick remains unaware of the initial trickery.*

[28–9] my will . . . ours   *what I want is that you should agree with our desire*

[36] attend   *wait for*

yet determined   *still resolved*

[38] hold my mind   *won't change my mind*

were she an Ethiope   *i.e. even if she were black. Not a happy comparison; a more acceptable meaning would be 'even if she were from the other end of the earth'.*

ANTONIO Which I will do with confirmed
    countenance.
BENEDICK Friar, I must entreat your pains, I think.
FRIAR To do what, signor?
BENEDICK To bind me, or undo me; one of them.   20
    Signor Leonato, truth it is, good signor,
    Your niece regards me with an eye of favour.
LEONATO That eye my daughter lent her; 'tis most
    true.
BENEDICK And I do with an eye of love requite her.
LEONATO The sight whereof I think you had from
    me,
    From Claudio and the Prince; but what's your
    will?
BENEDICK Your answer, sir, is enigmatical.
    But, for my will, my will is your good will
    May stand with ours, this day to be conjoined
    In the state of honourable marriage –   30
    In which, good Friar, I shall desire your help.
LEONATO My heart is with your liking,
FRIAR   And my help.
    Here comes the Prince and Claudio.

Enter DON PEDRO *and* CLAUDIO *with attendant lords*

DON PEDRO Good morrow to this fair assembly.
LEONATO Good morrow, Prince, good morrow,
    Claudio;
    We here attend you. Are you yet determined
    Today to marry with my brother's daughter?
CLAUDIO I'll hold my mind, were she an Ethiope.
LEONATO Call her forth, brother, here's the Friar
    ready.
                        [*Exit* ANTONIO

[41] February face   *Benedick is either maintaining his displeasure with Claudio, or preoccupied with other matters.*

[43] the savage bull   *A reference to their exchanges at I.1.257, and V.1.180–1, with the same bull/horns/cuckold association.*

[44] we'll tip thy horns with gold   *i.e. we'll make you a cuckold with real style (ambiguous: either he'll make a fine cuckold, or he'll be very thoroughly cuckolded)*

[45] Europa   *Europe, i.e. everyone*

[46–7] As once . . . in love   *The association of Europa and bull reminds Claudio of the story of Europa, the king of Phoenicia's daughter, who was abducted by Jove (see note at II.1.95–6) in the form of a white bull.*

[48] an amiable low   *a pleasant voice*

[49–51] And some . . . bleat   *Benedick implies that Claudio is the product of a similar union.*

[52] For this I owe you   *I'll pay you back later for this*
reckonings   *The debt metaphor again, as at IV.1.334 and V.4.9.*

[53] must seize upon   *The bald force of this contrasts with the language of love used in his wooing of Hero, and reveals an underlying resentment that honour coerces him to enter this unknown alliance.*

[54] and I do give you her   *Antonio seems to stress* give *to counteract the force of* seize.

[55] Sweet, let me see your face   *His urgent request betrays his anxiety about what is being required of him.*

[58–9] Give me . . . me   *He remains terse.*

DON PEDRO Good morrow, Benedick; why, what's
    the matter,   40
    That you have such a February face
    So full of frost, of storm and cloudiness?
CLAUDIO I think he thinks upon the savage bull.
    Tush, fear not, man, we'll tip thy horns with
      gold,
    And all Europa shall rejoice at thee,
    As once Europa did at lusty Jove
    When he would play the noble beast in love.
BENEDICK Bull Jove, sir, had an amiable low,
    And some such strange bull leaped your
      father's cow,
    And got a calf in that same noble feat   50
    Much like to you, for you have just his bleat.

Enter ANTONIO, *with the women masked*

CLAUDIO For this I owe you. Here comes other
    reckonings.
    Which is the lady I must seize upon?
ANTONIO This same is she, and I do give you her.
CLAUDIO Why then, she's mine. Sweet, let me see
    your face.
LEONATO No, that you shall not till you take her
    hand
    Before this Friar, and swear to marry her.
CLAUDIO Give me your hand before this holy Friar;
    I am your husband, if you like of me.
HERO [*Unmasking*] And when I lived, I was your
    other wife;   60
    And when you loved, you were my other
      husband.
CLAUDIO Another Hero?

[66] but whiles   *only as long as*
[67] All this amazement can I qualify   *i.e. I shall explain everything.* qualify: *moderate*
[69] largely   *in detail*
[70] let wonder seem familiar   *accustom yourselves quickly to the surprise*
[71] let us presently   *let's go straightaway*
[72] Soft and fair   *i.e. wait a moment*
[74] no more than reason   *no more than is reasonable*
[76] they swore you did   *(at II.3)*

[79] for they did swear   *(at III.1)*
[82] no such matter   *nothing of the kind*
[83] friendly recompense   *as a friend*

HERO   Nothing certainer.
　　One Hero died defiled, but I do live,
　　And surely as I live, I am a maid.
DON PEDRO The former Hero, Hero that is dead?
LEONATO She died, my lord, but whiles her slander
　　lived.
FRIAR All this amazement can I qualify
　　When after that the holy rites are ended,
　　I'll tell you largely of fair Hero's death.
　　Meantime, let wonder seem familiar   70
　　And to the chapel let us presently.
BENEDICK Soft and fair, Friar; which is Beatrice?
BEATRICE [*Unmasking*] I answer to that name. What
　　is your will?
BENEDICK Do not you love me?
BEATRICE   Why no, no more than reason.
BENEDICK Why, then your uncle, and the Prince,
　　and Claudio
　　Have been deceived; they swore you did.
BEATRICE Do not you love me?
BENEDICK   Troth no, no more than reason.
BEATRICE Why, then my cousin, Margaret and
　　Ursula
　　Are much deceived; for they did swear you did.
BENEDICK They swore that you were almost sick for
　　me.   80
BEATRICE They swore that you were well-nigh dead
　　for me.
BENEDICK 'Tis no such matter. Then you do not
　　love me?
BEATRICE No truly, but in friendly recompense.
LEONATO Come, cousin, I am sure you love the
　　gentleman.

[87] halting   *limping*

[88] Fashioned   *dedicated*

[91–2] Here's . . . hearts   *here our own writings bear witness against our professed feelings*

[93] I take thee for pity   *I'm only taking you out of pity*

[94] would not   *do not want*

[95] I yield upon great persuasion   *I'm only acquiescing under pressure*

[98] Peace . . . mouth   *In early editions, Leonato is given this line; he could well bring the two of them together to make them kiss, and end the wrangle. But it is probably better as Benedick's line since Leonato should refer to both of them, not just to one. It is also a neat parallel for Beatrice's injunction to Hero at II.1.306.*

[99] How dost thou   *how does it feel (to be)*

[101–2] a college of wit-crackers   *a whole school of jokers*

[102] flout   *mock*

humour   *(new) disposition*

[103] a satire or an epigram   *a mocking poem or witty saying*

[104–5] if a man . . . him   *if a man is going to allow himself to be defeated by such things, he ought to remain as unobtrusive as possible (to avoid comment and to avoid the attentions of women)*

[106] purpose   *intend*

[106–7] I will . . . it   *I shall take no notice whatever of what is said against it*

[108–9] therefore . . . against it   *don't bother to remind me of what I've said against it in the past*

[109] a giddy thing   *very changeable*

[109–10] and this is my conclusion   *and that's that*

[110–11] I did think to have beaten thee   *I had intended to hammer you (in the challenged fight)*

[111] like to be   *on the point of becoming*

[113] I had well hoped   *I was hoping*

[114–15] cudgelled thee out of thy single life   *beaten you (1) to death (2) out of being a bachelor*

CLAUDIO And I'll be sworn upon't, that he loves her,
 For here's a paper written in his hand,
 A halting sonnet of his own pure brain
 Fashioned to Beatrice.

HERO   And here's another
 Writ in my cousin's hand, stol'n from her
  pocket,
 Containing her affection unto Benedick.   90

BENEDICK A miracle! Here's our own hands against
 our hearts. Come, I will have thee; but, by this
 light, I take thee for pity.

BEATRICE I would not deny you; but, by this good
 day, I yield upon great persuasion. And partly to
 save your life, for I was told you were in a
 consumption.

BENEDICK Peace – I will stop your mouth. [*He kisses
 her*]

DON PEDRO How dost thou, 'Benedick the married
 man'?   100

BENEDICK I'll tell thee what, Prince: a college of wit-
 crackers cannot flout me out of my humour. Dost
 thou think I care for a satire or an epigram? No. If a
 man will be beaten with brains, 'a shall wear
 nothing handsome about him. In brief, since I do
 purpose to marry, I will think nothing to any
 purpose that the world can say against it; and
 therefore never flout at me for what I have said
 against it; for man is a giddy thing, and this is my
 conclusion. For thy part, Claudio, I did think to   110
 have beaten thee; but in that thou art like to be my
 kinsman, live unbruised and love my cousin.

CLAUDIO I had well hoped thou wouldst have denied
 Beatrice, that I might have cudgelled thee out of

[115] double dealer *(1) betrayer of your own convictions against marriage (2) a married man as opposed to a single one, and hence, potentially an unfaithful husband*

[116-17] look exceeding narrowly to thee *i.e. watch you like a hawk*

[120] and our wives' heels *i.e. in the dancing, and as a preparation for the wedding night (see III.4.45)*

[121] We'll . . . afterward *Leonato is justifiably anxious to complete the formalities first; Benedick is more confident.*

[122] music *musicians*

[124-5] There is . . . horn *the best way to command respect is to show you're experienced*

[124] staff *of office, symbol of authority*

reverend *worthy of respect*

tipped with horn *(1) old men's sticks were often decorated with horn (2) another reference to cuckold's horns*

[126-7] My lord . . . Messina *This news rounds off that part of the plot; and the unpleasant side of it is left until the next day.*

[129] brave *excellent (in the sense of suitable)*

pipers *the musicians for the dance*

[Dance] *To end with a full dance is entirely fitting as a symbol of harmony, and as a happy celebration of the play's resolution.*

thy single life to make thee a double dealer; which
out of question thou wilt be, if my cousin do not look
exceeding narrowly to thee.

BENEDICK Come, come, we are friends. Let's have a
dance ere we are married, that we may lighten our
own hearts and our wives' heels.   120

LEONATO We'll have dancing afterward.

BENEDICK First, of my word; therefore play, music.
Prince, thou art sad; get thee a wife, get thee a wife.
There is no staff more reverend than one tipped
with horn.

Enter a MESSENGER

MESSENGER My lord, your brother John is ta'en in
flight
And brought with armed men back to Messina.

BENEDICK Think not on him till tomorrow; I'll devise
thee brave punishments for him. Strike up, pipers.

Dance

[*Exeunt*